Their Jihad...
Not
My Jihad

Second Edition

This second edition of *Their Jihad... NOT My Jihad* was published by **Possibly Publishing**, which also publishes the trademark **How Can You Possibly**® book series.

For more information, please visit any of our websites:

www.howcanyoupossibly.com

email: **possiblypublishing@gmail.com**

Other titles by *Possibly Publishing*:

How Can You Possibly be a Muslim Feminist?

The Bully Grudge

How Can You Possibly be a Mormon and a Democrat?
Perspectives on Abortion, Economics, the Environment and Harry Reid

THEIR JIHAD... NOT MY JIHAD

Second Edition

BY
RAHEEL RAZA

FOREWORD BY
CLINTON JOE ANDERSEN, JR.

Their Jihad... NOT My Jihad
2nd Edition
by Raheel Raza
www.raheelraza.com

Foreword by Clinton Joe Andersen, Jr.

Copyright © 2011 by Raheel Raza

Raheel Raza retains all rights to publish and republish in any other format all of her works presented in this book.

Their Jihad... NOT My JihadPossibly Publishing
www.possiblypublishing.com
www.howcanyoupossibly.com

All rights reserved. No part of this book may be reproduced or transmitted in any form or by any means, electronic or mechanical, including but not limited to photocopying, recording or by any information storage and retrieval system, without written permission from the author, except for the inclusion of brief quotations for critical reviews.

ISBN 978-0-9819437-4-9

Publication of this Second Edition: September 15, 2012
Digital creation date 9/27/2012 10:24 AM

1 3 5 7 9 10 8 6 4 2

Design & Composition: Possibly Publishing
Cover design: Possibly Publishing
Cover Photo of Raheel Raza: Copyright 2008 by Raheel Raza

If God had so desired, he would have made everyone alike. But he has not done so that he may better test and try his people. In the meantime, compete with each other in good works. Upon your return to God, he will unravel the mystery behind your differences.
Qur'an 5:48

[A Catholic and an Anglican] seem to me most saintly men and to have loved God with their whole heart...

Nevertheless they disagree and (what racks and astounds me) their disagreement seems to me to spring not from their vices nor from their ignorance but rather from their virtues and the depths of their faith, so that the more they were at their best the more they were at variance.
C.S. Lewis

You open the newspaper to an article on some subject you know well. You read the article and see the journalist has absolutely no understanding of either the facts or the issues. Often, the article is so wrong it actually presents the story backward…

In any case, you read with exasperation or amusement the multiple errors in a story, and then turn the page to national or international affairs, and read as if the rest of the newspaper was somehow more accurate about Palestine than the baloney you just read.
Michael Crichton

Contents

FOREWORD: Where are the Muslim Serpicos? 1

INTRODUCTION: In Her Own Words 19
    An Open Letter to Osama Bin Laden 20
    Mischief in Manhattan (by Raheel Raza & Tarek Fatah) 23
    Merry Christmas from a Merry Muslim! 27

CHAPTER 1: Crises of Islam 33
    Faith and Love vs. Culture of Hate 33
    Muslims Need Tolerance and Sacrifice, Not Suicide 37
    Pakistan, A Country in Denial 43
    Loyalty to Our Adopted Land 49
    Reality Check on Security Checks 53
    A Call to Arms for Moderate Muslims 59
    Reducing God to a Policeman 65
    Order a Fatwa–Delivered in 30 Minutes or It's Free! 71
    American Muslim Convert Critiques Mosque Culture 75

CHAPTER 2: Images of Islam 79
    Understanding Jihad 79
    Oklahoma, When Will the Violence Stop? 83
    Their Jihad is NOT My Jihad 87
    Role of Media in Creating Peace 93
    Jihad in the Newsroom 99
    Are Our Civil Liberties at Stake? 107
    Do Muslims Eat Ketchup? 113

CHAPTER 3: Truths of Islam 125
    Need for Compassion and Tolerance 125
    Jesus in Islam 131
    Pursuing Peace through Education and Knowledge 135
    Building Religious Inclusivity 141
    The World Parliament of Religions–Pathways to Peace 149
    Beyond the Fluff Stuff 157
    Three Weddings and a Funeral 161
    What Led to the London Bombings? 165
    Eid and Awe in New York 169

A Free Gift from Raheel 177

    Brief Islamic Glossary 179
    Bibliography 181
    About the Author 183

FOREWORD

WHERE ARE THE MUSLIM SERPICOS?

I had never heard of Raheel Raza until September of 2010 when I stumbled across her August 9th interview with Bill O'Reilly, where she spoke out against building a mosque at Ground Zero. By the end of her interview, I was ecstatic to have found yet another answer to the question, "Where are the Muslim Serpicos?" This was a question raised and phrased by Dennis Miller on more than one occasion. I consider this question a fair one to ask.

The term "Serpico" is a reference to the New York City police officer, Frank Serpico, who fought police corruption in the 1960's. Miller's question implies that the corruption among the New York police culture at that time is analogous to the fanaticism currently at play in the Muslim world today.

What set Frank Serpico apart was not his refusal to take bribes. Certainly, he was not the only honest cop in town. The majority of police officers may have been honest, in that they did not take kickbacks nor actively participate in or benefit from the corruption that surrounded them. What made Serpico particularly courageous was his willingness to become a whistleblower. His peers would call him a "rat", of course. Not only does it mean testifying against your own but, when the corrupt are calling the shots, it means putting your life on the line. But that's what

Frank Serpico did. He put his life on the line by openly testifying against police corruption. And he paid a price for it by being shot in the face. He survived, however, and continued his fight against corruption. And his story was, eventually, dramatized in the 1973 film, *Serpico*, starring Al Pacino.

Within hours after the 9/11 attacks, Islamic organizations all around the world condemned the actions of the hijackers.[1] For example, Muhammad Sayyid Tantawi of the al-Azhar University Mosque in Cairo, Egypt had this to say on September 14, 2001:

> Attacking innocent people is not courageous, it is stupid and will be punished on the day of judgment. It's not courageous to attack innocent children, women and civilians. It is courageous to protect freedom; it is courageous to defend oneself and not to attack.[2]

Unfortunately, official condemnations were soon overshadowed by something much more dramatic: cheering and dancing in the streets.

The hijacked airplanes and thousands dead was the work of just a handful of men. Americans were not so ready to blame Islam for the actions of just a handful of Muslims. Unfortunately, when crowds of Muslims are caught on tape acting positively giddy at the sight of such death and tragedy, official condemnations are pretty meaningless. Muslims are going to need to produce quite a few Serpicos in order to overcome this PR nightmare.

---

[1] Hussain, *Security and Preparedness (2007 Chautauqua Lecture).*
[2] Tantawi, "Agence France Presse Newspaper Article."

In the meantime, we should take a moment and ask whether the footage of cheering in the streets gave us a false impression of how most Muslims actually reacted on 9/11. That's a tough question but a good place to start is to ask someone who was actually in the Muslim world on September 11, 2001.

In Yemen on 9/11

Peter Johnson is a filmmaker whose works include two recent documentaries *The Golden Road* and *Journey of Faith*, both of which involved shooting footage of the famed Incense Trail, which stretches eastward from the Mediterranean, across several countries of the Arabian Peninsula. This is how Peter Johnson and his crew found themselves in the country of Yemen during September of 2001. Johnson explains:

> We were unloading our equipment when Abdu came out of the lobby excitedly yelling, "An airplane has crashed into the White House!" We quickly went to our hotel rooms and watched in horror as the events of "9/11" unfolded before our eyes. It was late in the afternoon in Yemen, morning in New York City. We watched in astonishment as the planes hit the Towers. After a brief time to at least initially absorb what was happening in the United States, we gathered in one room to watch together and discuss what we should do. ... Yemen is the ancestral home of bin Laden, and the realization of where we were, in the midst of this shocking world event, started to sink in.[3]

---

[3] Brown and Johnson, *Journey of Faith*, 121–122.

Whenever I begin to relate Johnson's story to others, the most common question is, "Were the people dancing in the streets?" Yemen seems as likely a place as any other for people to put on a celebration. After all, they are very poor, very Arab, very Muslim and with strong ancestral ties to bin Laden, wouldn't you like to know how the people of Yemen reacted to the 9/11 terrorist attacks?

After the attacks, Johnson's crew was advised to stay away from large population centers until arrangements could be made to fly them out of the country, which would not happen for several days. But they were in a large population center on the day of the attacks. There were streets. There were people. So, were people dancing in these streets, as we repeatedly saw on the news? Was there any other sign of celebration?

The answer to that question is, NO! Not in Yemen.

On the contrary, the attitude of the majority of the Yemenese people that Johnson encountered was quite the opposite, as he explains:

> The morning after 9/11, I left my hotel room and went outside. We had a contingent of about 18 or so Yemeni military guards. And I walked over to the military commander and I looked at him (and I was trying to be as cheerful as one could be that morning) and... he looked at me and tears welled up in his eyes. And he said, "I'm so sorry." [4]
>
> He looked at me with genuine sorrow and expressed how bad he felt because of what had

---
[4] *A Filmmaking Odyssey: The Making of Journey of Faith.*

happened in America. I held his hand warmly and told him that we were very pleased to be in his fascinating country. I told him how much it meant to us to be with him and to see the land of his heritage. His eyes rimmed with tears, and he said, with emotion, that they were honored to have us with them. When I looked at the other soldiers, all their heads hung down. The commander saw this and said that they were "embarrassed" to face me. I asked him to tell his troops that we considered it a great blessing to be in Yemen and that it held great meaning for us. A smile came into his eyes and he seemed truly cheered by that. So many misconceptions about America exist in the Middle East. Many think that America hates them, and so they hate America in return. But their hatred for America does not necessarily mean they hate Americans. I found that sincere expressions of respect and affection from us warmed their hearts and ours immensely.[5]

How interesting that the Yemenese Military soldiers were so embarrassed that Johnson had to comfort and reassure **them**.

But what is clear from Johnsons account (and I have verified this with him personally) is that he saw no cheering or celebrating. None.

It Starts with an "I", Must it End with a "SLAM!"?

One of the most paradigm shifting books that I have ever read is *America Alone* by Mark Steyn. This book made me pay attention to demographics as a major

---

[5] Brown and Johnson, *Journey of Faith*, 118.

influence on world events. While I always recommend the preface[6] to *America Alone*, I do not like to recommend the entire book because Steyn always comes across a little too anti-Muslim. He too often referred to Islam as, "It starts with an **I** and ends with a **SLAM!**"

In his book, Steyn demonstrates that, as a group, Muslims are at least five times as reproductive as... well, everyone. This is particularly the case for European Muslims and other places outside the traditional "Muslim world". Basically, Steyn's premise is that the Muslim population is exploding and, as a result, they will become more populous and more powerful in the coming decades. They'll soon be an unstoppable voting block in Western Europe. Steyn paints a scary picture of the end of the world as we know it. Unfortunately, after illustrating this population shift, he just leaves us there... with all kinds of reasons to be scared of Muslims. And I think he misses an opportunity here.

As I see it, if the Muslim world is coming my way (my children's way), rather than be afraid of them, the wise course of action would be to learn all I can about Muslims. I've taken this to heart by asking a Muslim friend for a *Qur'an* and by visiting a local Mosque with my children. In fact, it makes all the sense in the world to have my children learn Arabic (not to mention Spanish and perhaps Chinese).

Seriously. The more familiar we can become with Muslim culture–not by just reading about them, but by interacting with Muslim neighbors–the less we

---

[6] Steyn, *America Alone*, xi–xxx.

will find ourselves in the dark and afraid of the future. You might even call this "pre-emptive reconciliation". And by reconciliation, I mean it in the sense given by the scholar Derek Evans:

> We should define "reconciliation" not as enemies coming to like each other, but as recognizing, whether we like it or not, we are in each other's future.[7]

You see, even if you view the Muslim population explosion as equivalent to an invading army, is it not all the wiser to learn the ways of Islam? We need not settle every difference. But we can remember that ignorance breeds fear because the enemy you know is much better than the enemy you don't.

So, like it or not, it seems beyond question that we are in each other's future. The real question for me and my children is, "Who will **we** choose to be in that future?" That is worth asking, particularly while we still have some time to influence the answer. It's something we ought to be doing whether there are Islamic Serpicos or not.

In the meantime, where are those Muslim Serpicos anyway?

Rwanda, Albania and Yemen on 9/11

I am pleased to say that, with very little effort, I have found more than a few Muslim Serpicos. However, since Serpico himself liked to use the term *lamplighters* to describe those "who seek truth and

---
[7] Evans, *Before the War*, 91.

justice in the face of personal risk", that's the term I will use. So, let's meet a few Muslim lamplighters.

Safety Amidst the Rwandan Genocide

At the time of the horrible genocides in the 1990s, Rwanda was perhaps the most Christian country in all of Africa, as a percentage of the total population. However, Christianity did not protect Rwanda from degenerating into a genocidal bloodbath, with neighbor against neighbor, teachers killing their students and vice versa, and even clergy killing those who sought sanctuary.[8] Dozens of priests, nuns and pastors have been charged and convicted of playing active roles in the mass killings,[9] including at least two priests who were executed for their crimes.[10]

Religion aside, most people are under the impression that these killings were driven by ethnic hatred alone, specifically Hutu vs. Tutsi. However, the motivations for the killings were not so cut and dry. For example, while the country as a whole lost about 11% of its population, even in a village where everyone was Hutu, at least 5% of its population were killed in the genocide.[11] Nevertheless, there were a few places, one in particular, where there were no killings whatsoever... and, chances are, you have never heard of it. There is a village just outside Rwanda's capital city of Kigali, a village where no one was killed. No one at all. And many potential

---
[8] Lacey, "Rwandan Priest Sentenced to 15 Years..."
[9] Nieuwoudt, "Rwanda: Church Role in Genocide Under Scrutiny."
[10] "Nun Convicted for Rwandan Genocide."
[11] Diamond, *Collapse*, 319.

victims found safe haven there. The place was called Biryogo.

What made that little corner of Rwanda an island of real peace and safety? There were a few factors, but they all seem to involve the fact that Biryogo was a Muslim village. The following excerpt tells the story:

> For nearly a century, Muslims remained on the fringes of Rwandan society. The faithful in Kigali were restricted to Biryogo, a dusty neighborhood where the Al-Fatah mosque now stands. They needed permits to leave.
>
> During the genocide, Muslims were among the few Rwandans who protected both neighbors and strangers. Elsewhere, many Hutus hunted down or betrayed their Tutsi neighbors and strangers suspected of belonging to the minority.
>
> But the militiamen and soldiers didn't dare go after Tutsis in Muslim neighborhoods like Biryogo, said Yvette Sarambuye, a 29-year-old convert.
>
> "If a Hutu Muslim tried to kill someone hidden in our neighborhoods, he would first be asked to take the holy *Qur'an* and tear it apart to renounce his faith," said Sarambuye, a Tutsi widowed mother of three who survived the slaughter by hiding with Muslims. "No Muslim dared to violate the holy book, and that saved a lot of us." [12]

A 35-year old Tutsi convert to Islam, named Jean-Pierre Sagahutu said that the Muslims in Rwanda

---
[12] Ngowi, "Rwanda Turns to Islam After Genocide."

do not view the world through a "racial or ethnic lens."

What remains a mystery to me still is why the Hutu extremists regarded the Muslims as such a group apart that the Hutu extremists were not to target them in the killings. You see, pygmies are also a group apart, in fact, a very distinct and ancient people throughout sub-Saharan Africa. In Rwanda, they are only about 1% of the population and have little political or economic power. So, even though pygmies were at the bottom of the socioeconomic ladder, hardly a threat to anyone, they were slaughtered at least as thoroughly as the rest of Rwanda's population.[13]

What then saved the Muslims in Biryogo and elsewhere in Rwanda? I can't say for certain. I can only hope to learn more as time goes on. Maybe it was a combination of fortunate circumstance. But I suspect that these were the natural consequences of practicing true religion. What I mean is, perhaps God protected the Muslims of Biryogo simply because they were practicing true Islam.

Rwandan Muslims Expel the Jihadists

Meanwhile, not long after the genocides, a group of Islamic fundamentalists (funded by a few wealthy Pakistanis) tried to establish themselves in Rwanda. They organized themselves to the extent that they had gained control of at least one Mosque. However, when there could no longer be any doubt about their philosophies and jihadist intentions, these Is-

---

[13] Diamond, *Collapse*, 318.

lamic fundamentalists were kicked out of the country by official Muslim organizations of Rwanda.[14]

So, whether the danger is massive genocide by Christians or the mere threat of imported Islamic fundamentalism, we now know that the Muslims in Rwanda not only practiced a "religion of peace" but they were also proactive by sheltering and protecting many others, whether Hutu or Tutsi, Christian or non-believer. Had there been any Jews in need of protection, they would have found it in Biryogo. I have no doubt about that because this protective behavior has precedence in Muslim communities throughout the world, from France to Albania.

Muslims Who Saved Jews in WWII

Most people are completely unaware that Muslims protected Jews from the Nazis in the period leading up to and during World War II. There is even a children's book called *The Grand Mosque of Paris*, which tells the story of how Muslims rescued Jews in Nazi occupied Paris.[15]

Another place where Jews found protection from the Nazis was in Albania, as told in a recent issue *Emel–The Muslim Lifestyle Magazine*:

> During that time of systematic persecution, it is nearly impossible to accept that there was one country in Europe that saw its Jewish population grow. But that is exactly what happened in Albania and Kosovo-Jews were safe there. Muslims ignored the grave risks to themselves and sheltered not only their Jewish

---
[14] Ngowi, "Rwanda Turns to Islam After Genocide."
[15] Ruelle and Desaix, *The Grand Mosque of Paris*.

neighbors, but also thousands of Jewish refugees fleeing Nazi terror. "During the Nazi occupation of Albania," states Johanna Neumann of the U.S. Holocaust Museum, "there is not one confirmed instance of a Jew being handed over to the Nazis by a Muslim Albanian."

The Albanian government actively defied Nazi rule. In 1938 King Zog, the first and only Muslim King of Europe, issued four hundred passports to refugee Jews, granting them safe entry into Albania. After learning of the Nazi campaign elsewhere in Europe, the Mayor of Tirane issued documents to Jewish families, protecting them by stating they were Muslims. When the Germans occupied Albania and demanded lists of Jews from the authorities, the Albanians answered, "We don't know any Jews, we only know Albanians." Everybody knew, but nobody told.

The Albanians' resistance is a hidden period in history, emerging now only after the fall of an isolationist communist regime. American photographer Norman H. Gershman has been exploring that tale. He is a long-time supporter of Yad Vashem (the Jerusalem-based Holocaust memorial), an organization that has honored more than 22,000 non-Jewish Holocaust-era rescuers. Gershman became fascinated by the little-known fact that Muslims had saved Jews, and decided to document their stories.[16]

By all means, buy Gershman's book, *Besa: Muslims who saved Jews in World War II*. It's filled with beautiful black and white photos of the heroic Muslims themselves and/or their children or grandchil-

---

[16] Emel Magazine, "When Muslims Saved Jews."

dren. Each photograph of these people is accompanied by their own story, told in their own words. It's the perfect coffee table book.[17]

Amin from Yemen

As already told, documentary filmmaker Peter Johnson and his crew found themselves stranded in the country of Yemen on 9/11. The crew had been advised to stay away from any population centers and even the American Embassy. It would be days before they could arrange to safely leave the country. In fact, the most pragmatic course of action was to head out into the desert and continue shooting footage of the terrain.

On September 12, 2001, shortly after sunset, the following occurred, as told by Peter Johson:

> On one of our stops, I was sitting in the Land Rover waiting for our journey to resume when I felt a hand touch my arm, which was resting on the open window. I looked to see one of our Bedouin guides, Amin, his face lit up with a warm smile. I turned to him as he took a ring from his hand and gave it to me to look at. It was a simple ring, not expensive. I turned it over in my hand, admiring it, and smiled back trying to express my appreciation for his friendship. Neither of us spoke the other's language, so body language was our only means of communication.
>
> After a moment, I handed the ring back to Amin, but he refused to take it. I tried again to give it back to him, knowing that he was a poor man, recently married, with few material pos-

---
[17] Gershman, *Besa: Muslims Who Saved Jews in World War II.*

sessions. Again, he refused and looked at me with the most compassionate countenance. He again gestured that he wanted me to keep the ring, his broad smile and earnest eyes lighting up his face with a bright, sympathetic expression.

I finally realized that Amin was attempting to let me know of his sorrow for the events of 9/11 and to assure me that he was my friend. I shall ever remember that moment in the stark desert when a very poor man reached across vast differences in culture, language, and religion to express his sincere brotherhood and love.[18]

The 2010 *Muslim Serpico Award* goes to...

Many Muslims came out in open opposition to the Ground Zero Mosque, among them was Canadian journalist Raheel Raza. On August 9, 2010, Bill O'Riley interviewed Raheel about her opposition to the mosque. Here are a few choice snippets from that interview:

O'Riley: Ms. Raza, why do you oppose building that mosque downtown?

Raza: I oppose the idea along with other members of the Muslim-Canadian Congress because it's confrontational. It is in bad faith. And it doesn't really set up any kind of dialogue or discussion on tolerance.

O'Riley: Well, the pro-mosque forces, including the mayor of New York City, say... the reason [for

---
[18] Brown and Johnson, *Journey of Faith*, 129.

	the mosque] is to show respect for the victims of 9/11. You're not buying that?
Raza:	No. As a Muslim, I'm not buying that at all. How does building a mosque in the very place where Muslims murdered so many other Americans... create any kind of respect?
	What I'm hearing from people, especially those who are victims... is that this is very hurtful, and it's very painful.
	As a Muslim, I read in my holy book, the Qur'an, that we should be very sensitive towards people of other faiths... and these are our neighbors and our colleagues and the people we care about.
	Building a mosque... across the street from Ground Zero is a slap in the face upon Americans. I can't begin to imagine how they would even conceive an idea that building a mosque there–an exclusive place of prayer for Muslims–would, in any way, build tolerance and respect.[19]

Pesonally, I never really had much of an opinion about the Ground Zero mosque. I still don't. I had always considered this issue to be the main concern of New Yorkers and the family of victims of 9/11. And yet I was startled by my own personal reaction to Raheel's words. To my surprise, I felt so consoled, as if I had been waiting for someone to come to my personal defense. A certain tension had lifted.

Ever since Dennis Miller issued the challenge, "Where are the Muslim Serpicos?" I had been confident they were surely out there. And I had found

---
[19] "Raheel Raza Interviewed by O'Reilly on Aug 9, 2010."

examples, in the past and across the world. But I had yet to witness a Serpico ***in action***, a live demonstration, if you will. But as I watched Raheel's interivew with O'Riley, I knew I had found my man, I had found my Serpico, all the braver because she is a woman.

Her next comment put her on another level:

> Mayor Bloomberg and other bleeding-heart white liberals like him don't understand the battle that we moderate Muslims are faced with in terms of confronting radical Islam and Islamization and political Islam in North America, which has only grown since 9/11 because of political correctness. People, because of their politically invested agenda, are not speaking out against issues like this.[20]

As a self-respecting conservative Republican, when she called Bloomberg a "bleeding-heart white liberal", I jumped out of my seat as if I had seen a touchdown. I admit it!

You see, though most people have trouble understanding Islam, these days, conservatives and Christians are especially shallow in their assessments. This is why I had been searching for a Muslim with the particular kind of ideology, one that would appeal to conservative Christians, in particular.

I don't know a thing about Canadian political parties or ideological terminology. And I don't technically know if Raheel Raza is or would consider her-self the American political equivalent of a "con-

---
[20] Ibid.

servative Tea Party Republican". But there's no doubt that calling Bloomberg "a bleeding-heart white liberal", would be a huge credential to many of those right-wingers who keep misunderstanding Islam.

So, right after I saw Raza's O'Reilly interview on YouTube, I searched for contact information and, the moment I found her phone number, I called her right then. She answered and...

A Personal Testimony of Her Relentless Optimism

So far as I could tell, nervous though I was, we had a most enlightening conversation. She quickly caught on to my idea of using a "How can you possibly..." question as the title of a book about Islam and terrorism. I hung up the phone thinking that she really did seem like an eternal optimist. Well, I didn't know the half of it.

You see, I found out much later that, apparently, during that first phone call, Raheel was afraid that I "might have been a wacko". Now, of course, her fears were alleviated a few months later when I sent her a prototype of the book (included this Foreword). But it was really after she recieved a simple hand written letter from my father that she came to understand the true roots of my motivations. It was then that she told me how her first impression of me was... less than perfect. And this really didn't surprise me.

However, to me this little incident illustrates the true meaning of "eternal optimist". Despite some initial feelings of trepidation on her part, she still gave me a very enthusiastic green light to produce a prototype of this book. Raheel is one woman that has reason to fear potential wackos. But she also understands the proper time and place for caution and the value in taking a chance and seeing where it leads. She took that chance with me and I shall be forever grateful.

Clinton Joe Andersen, Jr.

Introduction

In Her Own Words

Raheel defines her religious and political views online (on a popular social networking site) as follows.

Religious Views: *A non-sectarian progressive Muslim, sufi at heart, Christian and Jewish by origin as a child of Abraham, and culturally from the land of the Indus.*

Political Views: *Not Left, right or centre, just balanced moderation.*

The following three pieces are some of Raheel Raza's most interesting articles. They are a good sampler, as they reflect her inclusive attitude and her fearlessness, as well as her humor.

An Open Letter Osama bin Laden
Written by Raheel in September of 2001.

Mischief in Manhattan
Written by Raheel Raza & Tarek Fatah in August 7, 2010.

Merry Christmas from a Merry Muslim
A message that Raheel seems destined to write year around the holidays.

An Open Letter to Osama Bin Laden

September 2001

Mr. bin Laden:

Although you have no authority nor standing in my eyes to call an entire community to jihad, still I am taking up your call. Jihad is the "struggle of good over evil". Therefore, my jihad is to expose you and people like you, and to prove that you derive your convoluted knowledge of Islam and the Qur'an from sources known only to yourself. The jihad that you call "Holy war" is not mentioned anywhere in the Qur'an. However, I will draw your attention to the verse in which the merciful and compassionate creator of the Universe, Allah, has likened the killing of one person as "though he killed all of mankind".

You, Mr. bin Laden, are an evil person and the war you are waging now is neither holy nor justified. Nor were the acts of hijacking and terrorism anything else but wrong. According to Islam, an attack against innocent people is cowardice and an expression of rejection of God's blessings. That is, of course, the God that we believe in: the God of mercy and love.

Since you call yourself a Muslim and continue to use the name of God to invoke your horrific message, you must be aware that the Qur'an has an entire chapter devoted to the concept of "munafiq" (hypocrite).[21] History tells us that even 1,400 years ago, in the time of Prophet Mohammad (peace be upon him), there were

---

[21] Surah 63

elements within Islam, people who called themselves Muslim but caused more harm to Islam than the disbelievers. It was to warn the Prophet of such factors that God sent the verse to beware of the hypocrites.

You, Mr. bin Laden, as a true example of the Munifiqeen, have taken Islam back 1,400 years. You are nothing but a hypocrite trying to rouse ignorant people to acts of violence in the name of the same God who says so clearly in Qur'an: "O people we have formed you into nations and tribes so that you may know one another." (5:45)

Having said this, we also have something to thank you for. In your acts of senseless violence and madness, you have cleared the air for those Muslims who were confused. What you have done is shown very clearly to the world that there are two Islams being practiced today–one, the Islam of Prophet Mohammad– the Islam of peace and love, of forgiveness and compassion, of tolerance and spirituality, women's rights and equality. The other Islam is the militant, extremist, fanatic cult of those who misappropriate religious teachings to justify murder, inflict destruction on human society in the name of Shari'a, subjugate and suppress minorities and women to promote injustice, and have a philosophy that fellow Muslims who don't subscribe to their brand of religiosity are heretics. Having hijacked our faith, you have not only brought about the wrath of the people you call your enemy, but also the wrath of the true believers who believe in truth over lies, justice over injustice, bravery and chivalry over the cowardice of hurting innocent civilians, and the beauty of celebrating life as a blessing from God rather than ending it in a futile attempt to reach paradise.

Mr. bin Laden, you appear to give very compelling reasons for your actions. At the top of your list are your hatred of the West and its oppression of Muslim lands.

My questions for you are: Where were you when Saddam Hussein was torturing Muslims in Iraq? What have you done personally to alleviate the suffering of

Iraqi children? Did you or your organization al Qaeda build any hospitals, supply medicines or promote education in third world countries? Did you lobby to find a peaceful solution to the Palestine problem? And, instead of hiding like a mole under the hills of Afghanistan, why aren't you fighting this inane battle from the land of your birth instead of compromising the lives of innocent Afghani civilians who are already terrorized by your supporters–the Taliban?

Raheel Raza
A Muslim Woman Who Refuses to be Terrorized

Mischief in Manhattan

by Raheel Raza and Tarek Fatah
August 7, 2010

We Muslims know the Ground Zero mosque is meant to be a deliberate provocation. It's an act of "fitna"

Last week, a journalist who writes for the *North Country Times*, a small newspaper in Southern California, sent us an e-mail titled "Help." He couldn't understand why an Islamic Centre in an area where Adam Gadahn, Osama bin Laden's American spokesman came from, and that was home to three of the 9-11 terrorists, was looking to expand.

The man has a very valid point, which leads to the ongoing debate about building a Mosque at Ground Zero in New York. When we try to understand the reasoning behind building a mosque at the epicentre of the worst-ever attack on the U.S., we wonder why its proponents don't build a monument to those who died in the attack?

New York currently boasts at least 30 mosques so it's not as if there is pressing need to find space for worshippers. The fact is we Muslims know the idea behind the Ground Zero mosque is meant to be a deliberate provocation to thumb our noses at the "infidel." The proposal has been made in bad faith and in Islamic parlance, such an act is referred to as "Fitna," meaning "mischief-making" that is clearly forbidden in the Koran.

The Koran commands Muslims to, "Be considerate when you debate with the People of the Book" — i.e., Jews and Christians. Building an exclusive place of worship for Muslims at the place where Muslims killed thousands of New Yorkers is not being considerate or sensitive, it is undoubtedly an act of "fitna".

So what gives Imam Feisal Abdul Rauf [22] of the "Cordoba Initiative" and his cohorts the misplaced idea that they will increase tolerance for Muslims by brazenly displaying their own intolerance in this case?

Do they not understand that building a mosque at Ground Zero is equivalent to permitting a Serbian Orthodox church near the killing fields of Srebrenica where 8,000 Muslim men and boys were slaughtered?

There are many questions that we would like to ask. Questions about where the funding is coming from? If this mosque is being funded by Saudi sources, then it is an even bigger slap in the face of Americans, as nine of the jihadis in the Twin Tower calamity were Saudis.

If Rauf is serious about building bridges, then he could have dedicated space in this so-called community centre to a church and synagogue, but he did not. We passed on this message to him through

---

[22] Until the Ground Zero mosque controversy, Raheel Raza very much admired Imam Rauf. You can read her opinion in her 2005 piece entitled "Eid and Awe in New York", which is actually the very last article in this book. This disagreement illustrates the very simple fact that Muslims, like any other group of human beings, do, have always and will continue to disagree with each other, sometimes quite strongly. Islam is neither static or monolithic.

a mutual Saudi friend, but received no answer. He could have proposed a memorial to the victims of 9/11 with a denouncement of the doctrine of armed jihad, but he chose not to.

It's a repugnant thought that $100 million would be brought into the United States rather than be directed at dying and needy Muslims in Darfur or Pakistan.

Let's not forget that a mosque is an exclusive place of worship for Muslims and not an inviting community centre. Most Americans are wary of mosques due to the hard-core rhetoric that is used in pulpits. And rightly so. As Muslims we are dismayed that our co-religionists have such little consideration for their fellow citizens and wish to rub salt in their wounds and pretend they are applying a balm to sooth the pain.

The Koran implores Muslims to speak the truth, even if it hurts the one who utters the truth. Today we speak the truth, knowing very well Muslims have forgotten this crucial injunction from Allah.

If this mosque does get built, it will forever be a lightning rod for those who have little room for Muslims or Islam in the U.S. We simply cannot understand why on Earth the traditional leadership of America's Muslims would not realize their folly and back out in an act of goodwill.

As for those teary-eyed, bleeding-heart liberals such as New York mayor Michael Bloomberg and much of the media, who are blind to the Islamist agenda in North America, we understand their goodwill.

Unfortunately for us, their stand is based on ignorance and guilt, and they will never in their lives have to face the tyranny of Islamism that targets, kills and maims Muslims worldwide, and is using liberalism itself to destroy liberal secular democratic societies from within.

Merry Christmas from a Merry Muslim!

Earlier this year I received a lengthy letter from the town of Herouxville, Quebec. It was an explanation of their proposed policy on immigrants, integration and accommodation. Had I known this would become a hot topic during current elections, I might have saved the message, but I thought this was just another Quebec rant!

We should be thankful to the citizens of Herouxville for allowing this issue to become public because it clearly reflects the concerns of many Canadians. At a time when some mosque leaders are urging rejection of Canadian values and celebrations, this discussion becomes especially important for Canada's Muslim communities.

However, the residents of Herouxville did not present their case well and only succeeded in eliciting knee-jerk reactions. They talked of secularism and the banning of public displays of religion. They confused religion and culture and they obviously need to do some more homework. And I would like to help.

First, it should be clear that things like the Niqab (face covering), Burka, FGM[23] and honour killings are NOT Islamic. They are cultural practices, which have migrated into Canada with their host commu-

---
[23] Female genital mutilation.

nities. I believe such excess cultural baggage has no place in Canada, but banning such practices only takes them underground. There is much work to be done within immigrant communities to eradicate such ignorant practices, with full support of the mainstream.

Reasonable accommodation is a separate issue. In twenty years that I've been here, I've found Canadians to be accepting and accommodating by virtue of their polite nature. This is confirmed by the increase in places of worship, religious holidays, halal meat outlets and women wearing hijab in public. This reflects the general tolerance and respect, which has been the cornerstone of Canadian acceptance of Muslim immigrants.

Sometimes accommodation by the host community goes above and beyond. Sometimes it goes too far. Last week at a high-powered businesswomen's lunch, everyone enjoyed haute cuisine on china while I got an insipid halal meal complete with salad and desert in Styrofoam. I hadn't asked for it because it's easy to eat vegetarian or fish but I appreciate the thought!

> While everyone enjoyed haute cuisine on china, I got an insipid halal meal complete with salad and desert in Styrofoam.

Contrary to this, in some Muslim countries, Westerners don't have the same freedoms we enjoy in Canada and there's little or no accommodation for their religious and cultural needs. They have to follow the law of the land, no matter how oppressive. As a Muslim woman I find Canada gives me more freedoms than in Muslim lands where I've faced the wrath of religious police in

INTRODUCTION

Saudi Arabia and been harassed by rude officials in Pakistan.

So why do we complain when we're asked to adapt to our new home where most of us have come by choice? After all, accommodation is a two-way street–you accommodate, we adapt. Accommodation also places a huge responsibility on us, not to make a nuisance of ourselves. Being Muslim is not only about finding a space to pray, it's more about respect for those around us. If my religious freedom becomes a nuisance for others, it's no longer a freedom but a burden.

What then constitutes the fine line between reasonable accommodation and unreasonable demands? Reasonable accommodation is the multi-faith chapel at Toronto airport with a large section for Muslims; nuisance value is the airport employee who insists on a separate room allocated only for her. It's our responsibility to find time and space to pray, not our teachers, employers or colleagues. Reasonable accommodation is including Muslim books in the library; but demands to eliminate Three Little Pigs from the traditional story, are unreasonable.

> When liberal progressive Canadian Muslims are trying to make a dent in the dogma of rituals, it's important to note that instead of spending an inordinate amount of time on inane debates about the halal-ness of maple syrup, we should be engaged in pro-active dialogue.

At a critical time in our lives when liberal progressive Canadian Muslims are trying to make a dent in the dogma of rituals, it's important to note that instead of spending an inordinate amount of time on inane debates about the halal-ness of maple syrup, we should be engaged in pro-active dialogue and discussion about the future of our youth, public policies, elections and the security of Canada as we are an essential part of the multi-colored patchwork that makes this quilt so warm and welcoming.

Reasonable accommodation is celebrating our religious holidays with joy; unreasonable is the criticism of the mainstream to say Merry Christmas and celebrate their own culture.

So, just to be clear about things, I want to wish everyone a...

Merry Christmas from a Merry Muslim!

With the rapid spread of foot-in-mouth disease by the religious right and the righteously religious from Washington to Waterloo via Vancouver, I can't think of a better time to come out of the closet as a Merry Muslim.

To acknowledge that I love this time of year and have already been an active participant in the launch of the Christmas season is challenging to say the least. I say Merry Christmas with feeling since I recently celebrated my own festival of Eid on November 15, wished my Hindu and Sikh friends a delightful Diwali on November 12 and was invited to a Hanukkah celebration this week. So I feel I can participate in celebrations for Christmas with my Christian colleagues and friends who, we should remember, form the majority in Canada.

Before people get their knickers in a knot and slap fatwa #2 on my head (I received fatwa #1 last year for celebrating the birth of my own Prophet), let me clarify that I indulge in celebrations of the cultural and non-alcoholic kind, keeping my feet firmly grounded in my own faith. In fact, it is because of my religious convictions that I feel it is important to greet others on their day of celebration.

Last month, the Ontario provincial plaque marking the hundredth anniversary of the Santa Claus Parade was unveiled, and I was front and centre as a volunteer. Wrapped in my deepest red shawl, red jingly reindeer antlers perched on my head, I spent the afternoon in Toronto's Nathan Philips Square shaking my bells to Christmas carols sung by the St. Michael's Choir School.

I was honored to be part of this event, which highlighted the history of the parade. It was delightful to see and feel the enthusiasm of the choir, a multicultural group of young, talented kids who were my responsibility to organize. When the surprise guest, Santa, emerged from Toronto City Hall, I cheerfully posed for photos.

This is when I was fondly dubbed the Merry Muslim, which I take as a compliment since I have long tried to get everyone to say "Merry Christmas" instead of "Happy Holidays".

A Muslim friend who is an elementary school principal decorates her office and talks during assembly about each specific holiday as it is observed. This, she says, is like anti-racism instruction and a lesson in world religions. From aboriginal students to Zoroastrians, everyone's culture and faith is celebrated, including, of course, Christmas. She admits it is a lot of work, but it keeps her school in a constant state of celebration. How inspiring. I wish we did this in our workplaces where people get hot under the collar over calling things by their proper names. I am on the committee organizing our Christmas celebration at work–and I refuse to call it anything other than Christmas.

Ironically, my colleagues on the committee are all Christians who are trying to convince me that calling our event a Christmas party won't be acceptable to all. I remind them that people around the globe, from Afghanis to Zambians, call December 25 Christmas, whether they celebrate it or not.

So please, let's call Christmas by its real name. By sharing one another's faith and culture, we can promote goodwill and good cheer.

> I have long tried to get everyone to say "MERRY CHRISTMAS" instead of "HAPPY HOLIDAYS".
> Let's call Christmas by its real name. By sharing one another's faith and culture, we can promote goodwill and good cheer.

CRISES OF ISLAM

Faith and Love vs. Culture of Hate
November 2001

Among the many e-mails being forwarded on the Internet post-September 11, one struck a strong chord. This is from an American, who asks,

> Why should I be the target audience of what 'true' Islam is? I don't need to know... tell the Muslims who have their *Qur'an* and *Sunnah* all backwards... I don't want to hear the history of the Crusades or U.S. foreign policy and the C.I.A... Why is there no overt and highly visible attempt to re-educate error-laden believers to the 'true' message of Islam and Prophet Mohammad? I'm confused.

She's not the only one. Some Muslims are confused, too–especially those who understand that it's no longer an issue of "blame-the-victim" or devious political conspiracies. The message is clear that many Muslims are not practicing the faith the way it was taught by Mohammad–so we have to find a solution within Islam.

While some voices are heard, reproving the misuse of Islam, we have to go a few steps further and actually implement solutions. Those countries or individuals who acquiesce to acts of terror, or worst still, give tacit approval to violence or murderous acts in the name of God, have to be strongly criticized and condemned.

This is not an easy task when fanatics and extremists have already hijacked our faith and when moderate voices are not heard over the babble of hate-mongering. Granted, the Muslim majority is not prone to violence and fanaticism, but many of us are to blame for remaining quiet and allowing religious zealots to practice various forms of terrorism within Muslim societies without fear of punishment or retaliation.

For example, Pakistan, which is currently prominent as an ally, has harboured and promoted domestic terrorism for the past two decades. In Pakistan, anyone with a weapon has the freedom to kill another human being without fear of reprisal. There is no accountability, so no one gets caught, let alone punished. Sectarian violence, in which Muslims have killed Muslims of other sects in the name of God, has been rife. Fortunately, everyone who is sane agrees that Pakistan President Pervez Musharraf is now in a pivotal position to change the course of events in his country–both politically and religiously.

As a result of regulations like the Blasphemy Law, minorities like the Ahmeddiya have been persecuted. (The form for passport issuance and renewal in Pakistan needs the applicant to sign a statement to the effect that the Ahmeddiya community is not part of Islam.) The Christian community in Pakistan is one of the most peace-loving and passive communities that has lived in harmony with its fellow Pakistanis for many years. Sadly, the recent massacre of 18 Christian worshippers in Bahawalpur, Pakistan is only one example of ongoing genocide. Ironically, Pakistan was built on the foundation of Islam–the true face of Islam that grants freedom and protection to minorities.

So where did all this bigotry come from? Intolerance and persecution of minorities came about due to a culture of hate and violence, which was allowed to permeate places of worship. Instead of expressing the message of tolerance and love, which is essential to Islam, a convoluted message of hate and venom has been sent forth. Unfortunately, few speak out against these atrocities and if they do, they are quickly silenced.

What needs to be done? The solution, I believe, lies with the silent majority in Islam who need to speak up and ensure the

> Whether this is done through the law, state or a group of individuals, removing such criminals should be swift and supported by all Muslims if they want to ensure the sanctity of Islam...

hateful rhetoric and actions of people like Osama bin Laden and his supporters die before they take root. They need to ensure the pulpit of a mosque is not used to spew hate, and most of all, they need to empower other Muslims to take action against injustice, intolerance and violence wherever it is happening. Whether this is done through the law, state or a group of individuals, the acts of removing such criminals should be swift and supported by all Muslims if they want to ensure the sanctity of Islam the way it was taught by the Prophet. We must reiterate that Islam was and should remain a message of peace and love.

The few of us who do speak out will face resistance and criticism. But maybe what we need right now is a renaissance or revival in Islam to clean out the extremist elements that have muddied our clean image. For this to happen, we have to first accept that the enemy is not outside, but within us. Islam has a history of those who have harmed the faith from within. These people are called "munafiq" or hypocrites and a message was sent to the Prophet Mohammad, warning him against the munafiq who cause more harm to the faith than anyone from the outside could ever accomplish.

Osama bin Laden and those who propagate a culture of hate and violence are perfect examples of such hypocrites and need to be exposed, condemned and charged. This will not happen with weapons and missiles–it has to happen through political strength and the might of the Muslim world, which can wield a strong influence on those who have the capabilities to find and eradicate terrorism.

It is about time Muslims stopped living in denial, woke up and started publicly and privately taking action against those who blatantly and brazenly misuse our faith.

Simultaneously, Muslims have to empower foreign governments who support and finance countries like Pakistan to ensure the aid is contingent upon restoration of human rights and the eradication of domestic terrorism.

Muslims Need Tolerance and Sacrifice, Not Suicide

March 2002: Advent of the Islamic New Year

Infuse your heart with mercy, love and kindness for your subjects... either they are your brothers in religion or your equals in creation.
    Caliph Ali bin Abu Talib (d. 661)

The Islamic New Year (a lunar calendar ten days short of the Gregorian) is called Moharram. This is a time for deep reflection and retrospection for Muslims worldwide and tells of one of the most significant events of sacrifice in Muslim History. This is the sacrifice of Imam Hussain, grandson of the Prophet Mohammad, for good over evil. Throughout this month, stories are retold of the importance of sacrifice and tolerance, two essentials of Islam that many of us seem to have forsaken.

In the West, Islam is generally looked upon as a religion of force and violence and regarded as being very intolerant. It is unfortunate that incidents like the horrific massacre of Christians in an Islamabad mosque and the alarmingly frequent crimes of suicide bombers only fuel this image. Despite extremist criminal actions, Islam is essentially a faith of peace and tolerance.

In the Encyclopedia Americana, the meaning of tolerance is to bear, to endure, to put up with. In recent times, however, the meaning and range of the subject have changed. There is no equivalent term in the Arabic language to mean what is traditionally understood in English by tolerance. The word that is used in Arabic is *tasamuh*. The root form of this word has two connotations–generosity and ease. Thus, for Muslims, tolerance indicates generosity and ease from both sides on a reciprocal basis. Tolerance is the cornerstone of Islam and has emerged out of the very nature and history of Islam. Being the youngest of the three monotheistic faiths, the Qur'anic revelation came at a time when Christians and Jews were already practicing their faith and living with the Muslims.

> Recognizing that Christians and Jews were faithful people, the Qur'an called them *ahl-al-kitaab* or people of the book.

Recognizing that Christians and Jews were faithful people, the *Qur'an* called them ahl-al-kitaab or people of the book (the book being the *Torah* or the *Bible*). Traditionally, Muslims did not view Christians and Jews as minorities in the way that other religions in the West are now described.

The *Qur'an*, therefore, proactively discusses relationships with non-Muslims as well as giving direction as to how Muslims should treat others around them.

Through the *Qur'an*, God addresses all people and says:

> *O mankind, we created you from a single pair of a male and female and made you into nations and tribes so that you may know each other. Verily the most honored of you in the sight of God is the*

most righteous of you, and God has full knowledge and is well acquainted with all things. (HQ 49:13)

The diversity of races, colors and creeds in the world are seen as a sign of God's blessing and should lead to closeness rather than racism and intolerance. Therefore, tolerance has been a natural, inseparable part of Islam from the beginning. Muslims did not tolerate non-Muslims grudgingly, but welcomed them to live feely in Muslim society, giving them protection and not forcing them to fight their battles. At the height of Islam's success, the *Qur'an* set the principle of "there is no compulsion religion" as well as "to me my religion, to you is yours."

The *Qur'an* affirms that God has created people to be different and that they will always remain different not only in their appearance but also in their beliefs. Unity of humans does not necessarily mean uniformity. The *Qur'an* refers to the people of the book in a positive light. It says:

They are not alike. Of the people of the book there is a staunch community who recite the revelations of God in the night season, falling prostrate before him. They believe in God and the last day and enjoin right conduct and forbid indecency and vie with one another in good works. These are of the righteous. (HQ 3:113)

Similarly, the *Qur'an* allows Muslims to eat the food of the people of the book and to marry their women.

Referring to the Prophets that came before Mohammad, the *Qur'an* says "Muhammad is but a messenger, before whom other messengers were sent." The *Qur'an* also guides Muslims to appeal to the people of book through what is common between them. The *Qur'an* says,

> *O people of the book—come to common terms as between us and you: that we have to worship none but God, that we associate no partners with him, that we erect not from among ourselves Lords and patrons other than God. (HQ 3:64)*

In the *Qur'an*, God addresses Muslims and the followers of other religions, saying, "We have ordained a law and assigned a path to each of you. Had God pleased he could have made you one nation, but it is his wish to prove you by that which he has bestowed upon you. Vie then with each other in good works, for to God you shall all be returned and he shall declare to you what you have disagreed about."

This direction to leave differences to be settled on the Day of Judgment is repeated many times in the *Qur'an*. Even in their relations with polytheists, who stand as the extreme opposite of the Islamic belief in monotheism, Muslims are instructed in the *Qur'an*:

> *God does not forbid you to be kind and equitable to those who do not fight for you or your faith and do not drive you out of your home. For God loves those who are just. (HQ 60:8)*

The *Qur'an* further instructs Muslims not to argue with the people of the book and to deal with them in a fair way. The *Qur'an* advises Muslims to say to the people of the book,

> *We believe in what has been revealed to us, and in what has been revealed to you. Our Lord and your Lord is one and the same and to him we submit ourselves. (HQ 3:84)*

When the Muslims of Arabia, under their ruler, Caliph Umar, entered Jerusalem (then called Aeilia) in 638 AD, Umar made the following agreement with the inhabitants, in accordance with Qur'anic injunctions:

> This is the security which Umar, the servant of God, the commander of the faithful, grants to the people of Aeilia. He grants to all, whether sick or sound, security for their lives, their possessions, their churches and their crosses, and for all that concerns their religion. Their churches shall not be changed into dwelling places, nor destroyed nor the crosses of the inhabitants, nor aught of their possessions, nor shall any constraint be put on them in matters of faith, nor shall any of them be harmed.

This was modeled on the life of the Prophet as he followed the command of God through the *Qur'an*. Muslims allowed non-Muslims to live in accordance to their customs even if these were forbidden in Islam. Thus, Christians were allowed to breed pigs, eat pork and make and drink alcohol in Muslims countries, even though these are forbidden to Muslims.

Today, tolerance refers to tolerating people, beliefs and traditions that are different from one's own. While globalization enhances this cause, it is also heightened by the lack of religion in people's lives around the world. Sometimes tolerance in current terms refers to political correctness. However, the Islamic ideal is not to just accept, but to embrace those who are different without compromising one's own principles.

Islam ordains enjoining the good and forbidding what is wrong and does not allow practices that fundamentally undermine the family system. For example, it would not recommend campaigning for the decriminalization of drugs.

Muslims are under obligation not to force their religious norms on others; to live under the law of the land, provided it does not go against the principles of Islam.

Pakistan, A Country in Denial

May 2002

Since my arrival to Canada in 1989, I have returned to visit Pakistan, my land of birth, at least once a year. My visits help me to stay in touch with my roots and also allow me to keep a keen eye on the political pulse of this volatile country.

As I traveled to Karachi a few weeks ago, I was a bit apprehensive because post-9/11, Pakistan has been in the eye of the storm. Pakistanis in North America, shaken to the core, have been galvanized into dialogue, discussion and forums. I was curious to learn how people in Pakistan were reacting.

The mood is strange and unnatural for a country on the brink of nuclear war, faced with a massive crisis within its own ranks and a raging war in the neighborhood. One section of the community, mostly the educated elite, is in complete denial, living in their own little elite world. They talk of designer outfits, jewelry and decadent parties.

At one Pakistani wedding, close to 10 tons of fresh flowers were purchased for just one ceremony and then left to rot on the street. It is typical for wedding clothing to cost anywhere from $1,150 to $1,750 per ensemble–and that is just for the guests! The bride's designer outfit can cost from $5,800 to $23,250.[24]

---

[24] These are in 2002 Canadian Dollars (CDN).

The price tags are staggering, considering the average annual income in Pakistan is $490 per year. Thirty-five percent of the population lives below the poverty line.

With this crowd, there's no chance of a conversation about the realities of life or grass roots issues like human rights.

As a guest in my sister's home, I felt a bit decadent, attended by two cooks, two maids, two chauffeurs and two gardeners! I mentioned this to my sister and she justified the need for double caretakers as she has two daughters-in-law living with her. I think the real reason is that young people in upper middle class homes can't carry a dish to the sink or (God forbid) clean bathrooms. The worst day of their lives is when servants don't turn up for work. The servant problem is an issue high on the priority list.

> I had been warned not to venture into deep water. I think my family was concerned that I might say something controversial and spoil their social standing. Me, controversial?

I managed to hold my tongue and not rock the boat. After all, it's a great holiday when one is not involved in any physical or mental exercise. I was served tea in bed everyday; was offered a menu of choices for lunch, tea and dinner; read magazines; had a facial; saw what privileged people in third world countries do for leisure; and generally soaked up the "club culture". After three days, I was ready to climb the walls so I found a computer and logged onto world news.

My only intellectual stimulation was an invitation to speak at the Rotary Club in Karachi. I was to speak of my involvement in interfaith outreach in Canada. On the day of my talk, I donned my public speaker cap and checked my notes for signs of blasphemy. I had been warned not to venture into deep water. I think my family was concerned that I might say something controversial and spoil their social standing. Me, controversial?

I was thrilled to see that a Canadian Rotarian from Trenton was visiting and came to hear me speak. Just as well; I think he was the only one among 50 other men and two women in the audience who appreciated and understood what I said. He announced I was a great ambassador for Canada, a comment that jarred with my audience because it is difficult for them to accept that I can be a pluralist practicing Muslim and a caring Canadian simultaneously.

My topic was about human rights, tolerance and the importance of interfaith outreach post-9/11, especially with Christians and Jews whom we consider to be from the same Abrahamic root and people of the book. The only other woman in the audience (one was my sister who was so stressed over my address that she didn't eat her lunch) wrote me a note saying that I am wrong: Islam is the only true Abrahamic faith and no one else will find salvation. This is the religious mood of majority of Pakistanis, irrespective of their social or economic status–dangerously exclusivist and holier-than-thou.

My touch on tolerance was shattered to the core as soon as I left the Rotary event. Newspaper headlines screamed the daylight shooting of Daniel Pearl, and a Shia doctor, head of the Kidney Center, father of two and twentieth in a line of innocent Shia doctors massacred since January 2002. It felt like a personal blow. But worse than the act itself was the feedback and justification. Most people told me I was over-reacting because I've become too Westernized. "Pakistanis could never do this–it's aliens," they said. "You don't know–Daniel Pearl was a spy." I felt sick and caustically congratulated them for having advanced from "Zionist" or "Indian conspiracies" to this "artificial intelligence" idea.

The other section of the community, the common man on the street, is totally confused about supporting the liberal view of the present government and being labeled "secular" (which is like abuse) or following the hate-spewing Mullah in the mosque. The masses have been brainwashed into justifying terrorism and blame everyone else for the problems facing Pakistan today. In an atmosphere rampant with stereotypes of "the West", America is the common enemy of both the elite and the masses.

However, their hypocrisy and double standards are soon revealed as they flaunt their Western ideals. On Valentine's Day, the city of Karachi floated red balloons and even the simple flower vendor at the street corner was caught up in the hype, stringing together garlands of hearts. Kids at school wore red and parents blamed it all on the West. Similarly, when they eat at McDonald's and Kentucky Fried Chicken, they still gripe at the West but have no qualms about vacationing in Florida or lining up for days so their two-year-old children can get admission at The Karachi Grammar school, a Western symbol that raises status. It is also a status symbol to send kids to The American School or spend millions of rupees to educate them in America.

While I'm deeply troubled and saddened by the lack of personal accountability in Pakistan, I continue to love my country of birth (like a spoilt child) and will return whenever I can. I only criticize because I care.

Thoughts on the Destruction of My Homeland

When will it end...this massacre and carnage–the blood,
*   sweat and tears of our young and old?*
When will we learn to live without fear... embedded deep
*   in our soul–with blood turned cold?*
When will we stop destroying each other... victims of the
*   enemy who has become bold?*
When will we say... peace in my land–I want to go home?

Loyalty to Our Adopted Land
December 2003

Abdulrahman Khadr's picture on the front page of *The Toronto Star* touches my heart. Bright-eyed, clean cut and 20, the same age as my older son, he looks like an average Canadian youth. But something seems to be amiss.

While my two boys learned to load the dishwasher, Khadr learned to load an assault rifle. While, much to my annoyance, my boys played violent video games, Khadr was actually living among people who practice violence against women and minorities. When I proudly took my kids on their first trip to Disneyland, Khadr was proudly sent to a training camp in Afghanistan. When my boys went to Sunday school in Brampton to learn their Islam, Khadr was being taught in a land far away. There's something terribly wrong with this picture, and I'm trying to make sense of it.

My concern as a Muslim mother is that Khadr seems to take all this in stride. He says that he and an older brother took training because it was "a normal thing that everybody does in Afghanistan". That may be so. But is it normal for Canadian Muslims to send their kids to learn violence and destruction in a camp thousands of miles away?

When my children came as young kids to Canada, their father and I taught them about loyalty to their adopted land and respect for the Canadian Charter of Rights and Freedom, which is not at odds with our Muslim values. We also made it a point to take them back regularly to Pakistan, our country of origin, so that they would know their roots and become culturally aware.

At one point, my younger son, at age 18, wanted to join the Canadian armed forces. I asked him, "If Canada were by chance to go to war against the land of your parents' birth, where would your loyalties lie?" Without the flicker of an eyelash, he said, "Canada, of course." I didn't reprimand him because he "stands on guard" for Canada.

Much of the onus and responsibility about what happens with our children's future lies with the parents. In a country like Canada, there are ample opportunities to help those in distress and those living in war-torn countries through valid means. Doctors Without Borders is a perfect example. I feel sorry for Muslim youth like Khadr, who haven't been taught that Islam means peace and submission to the will of God–not submission to the call for violence being spouted by some malicious Mullahs.

If parents are naïve and don't watch what their children are absorbing, then unfortunately, we will have produced many Khadrs in our society. It's easy to become prey to the emotional call for a physical jihad as many Muslim youth, born and bred in England, have done in the recent past. They were sucked into the vortex of an ideology gone mad and never told that the larger jihad is that of tolerance and understanding. I often wonder about those who entice youth to commit suicide bombing. We don't see any of those who preach suicide bombing throwing themselves in front of a bus.

CHAPTER 1: CRISES OF ISLAM

Khadr's case is a huge wake up call for all Canadian Muslims. This could happen to our kids. But we hope it won't because we are vigilant about what they learn, about teaching them inherent Muslim values and applying them in the Canadian context.

As the web of hatred increases from East to West and people find trouble with religion, we try to build bridges and steer our family away from the ritual to the spiritual, finding truth not only in the *Qur'an* but in messages of peace and justice emanating from all faiths.

Hate and racism are taught at home and children take example from their parents. From the fall of the Buddha statues in Afghanistan to the burning of libraries in Iraq, we as a family have lobbied against injustice and shared our joys and sorrows with our friends of all faiths.

> They were sucked into the vortex of an ideology gone mad and never told that the larger jihad is that of tolerance and understanding.

We enjoy a langar (meal) in a Sikh Gurdwara on Dixie Road in Mississauga, Ontario as much as we appreciate answering tough questions about Islam in Canadian churches or synagogues.

I wonder if those who have enormous resentment in their hearts ever had the pleasure of driving along the "spiritual strip" on Bayview Avenue in Toronto where a Chinese temple, Christian churches, a Zoroastrian temple, a mosque and a synagogue stand side by side. If they did, they would be awed by the beauty and tolerance that lies at the heart of Canada.

Reality Check on Security Checks
February 2004

I went for my flu shot this morning, registered at the reception desk and sat to wait my turn. About five minutes later I noticed that four people (all white) who had come after me got called in while I still waited. "Aha," I thought, "there's racial profiling going on here."

My conclusion had much to do with my reading the newspaper, which abounds with material on this hot topic. However, I decided to stay cool and after the fourth person went ahead of me, I asked the receptionist what the matter was. She was mortified to discover that she had missed my name on the list and apologized so profusely that I felt embarrassed. The incident made me realize that it's easy to make an issue about racial profiling. In this case, it was simple human error. Racial profiling, racism and discrimination are real concerns but they are sometimes fuelled by our own perceptions.

Some form of racial profiling exists in every part of the world–I've lived in the Arab world long enough to know that priorities there are Whites, Arabs and Asians in terms of jobs, visas and attitude. Some Middle Eastern countries are paranoid about security and use very elementary methods of implementing them. But many of us accept these restrictions because we expect them.

Rohinton Mistry, a respected Canadian writer, cancelled his trip to the U.S. because he felt American security inspections were degrading. The Indian-born Canadian, who is not Muslim, claimed he endured "unbearable humiliation" due to racial profiling. Mistry remarked, "The way you look, where you were born... will determine how you will be treated at certain airports."

Yes, he is absolutely right, but those "certain airports" are not only in the U.S.

I'll never forget my last visit to Saudi Arabia. They treat you like dirt if you're Asian. I remember standing in a long line with two kids, hungry and tired while the customs officer sipped tea and chatted with his friends, calling out those passengers who had British or American passports. When we finally made it to the front of the line, he left our passports on the counter and went away for a break without so much as an explanation. Our luggage was searched and the cover torn off a book because it had the photo of a woman. The attitude was so harsh that as a Muslim, I vowed that the only reason I would ever go there again would be to visit the holy shrines.

On my return from Pakistan recently, I had an unnerving experience at Karachi airport. My luggage was searched by two men, put through an x-ray device and, finally, it was machine bound by a metal strip for good measure. Then I went through a strict immigration check where I was photographed. Two steps later, I was stopped by an obnoxious and arrogant Federal Investigation Agency agent who rudely questioned my status as a woman traveling alone. He wanted to confiscate my Canadian passport until I told him whether I had a husband or father in Canada. When I protested loudly that it was

CHAPTER 1: CRISES OF ISLAM

none of his business, I was almost arrested. Being surrounded by a dozen gun toting, rough-looking army guys is no joke! I was shaken to the core.

Just before boarding the plane, we went through security again and this time, a woman felt me all over as part of the body search! I couldn't yell racism because these were my own people. I justified this horrific experience by saying they were doing their job of handling security the only way they knew how.

I returned to Toronto via London where there was intense screening and long lines, shoes on one side and passengers on the other, while the customs officers searched all hand luggage. I went through all sorts of machines along with other passengers. The British are not rude, but quite brusque. No one complained.

> Why is it so difficult for the average traveler to accept that the Americans have a right to tighten their security and obviously target those of ethnic origin who come from countries that the terrorists boasted to be from?

People are complaining that U.S. security is stringent. However, it wasn't too long ago that there was an invasion of security in America, where thousands of civilians were brutally killed in a non-combative attack. The terrorists were from different parts of the world. A few months later a shoe bomber nearly blew up a plane. Why is it so difficult for the average traveler to accept that the Americans have a right to tighten their security and obviously target those of ethnic origin who come from countries that the terrorists boasted to be from?

In the past year, I've made numerous trips to the U.S. and have never been mistreated at a US airport. I've been delayed and searched, but not singled out despite my ethnic appearance, nose ring and birthplace on the passport. Recently, my husband and I were in Denver, Colorado, which has a huge airport. Prior to our departing flight, everyone had to go through intense security. It took 45 minutes and was extremely well organized. Security personnel were polite and well informed; they told everyone what was happening at every step and said please and thanks. If they had to search your person, they actually made a statement before touching you.

There was only one seat on the flight back to Toronto so my husband had to stay back and for a moment I was worried. He sports a beard, looks like he is from the Middle East and was born in Pakistan so he has "the profile". Sohail told me he couldn't have been treated better. Not only did airport personnel work at getting him on another flight to Toronto right away, they apologized profusely for something that wasn't their fault. He had to come via Chicago, another huge airport where security is very rigid. However, Sohail went through the process with many others and he argues that he was the one whom most security personnel apologized to. Likely, the polite treatment was because Sohail refrained from letting off his frustration in being delayed onto the security personnel, recognizing they were doing the best they could.

There are exceptions to the rule, of course. Even in normal times, there are bigots and people with a personal axe to grind. Racism and discrimination do exist. These, however, are not normal times for the U.S. While clarifying that I have no love lost for President George W. Bush or American foreign policies, I believe the U.S. has reason to be cautious. At security checks, if one observes carefully, without a chip on the shoulder, then it becomes apparent that black, brown and white people are randomly stopped and searched. If those of Middle Eastern descent are searched more than others, then maybe the U.S. has good reason to do so. If the angst against airport security checks in America is so great, we can either get used to it or stop going there.

A Call to Arms for Moderate Muslims
April 2004

The recent raids in Britain that resulted in the arrests of nine men of Pakistani heritage and the subsequent raid at the home of a Canadian in Ottawa are cause for grave concern. Concern, not just about the credibility of the Royal Canadian Mounted Police, (after their bungling over the arrest of 19 Pakistani students where no terrorism charges were proven), but concern about the future of Muslims in Canada.

As a Muslim Canadian, my work within and outside my community has suddenly become an enormous challenge.

The other day, I was invited to address a church group in Etobicoke, Ontario as part of my interfaith outreach. The topic, naturally, was Islam. The audience was familiar with the basics of Islam. They were more interested in knowing how I, as a Canadian Muslim, experience religion in my life and how Islam relates to other faiths.

I spoke about the Islam that I love and respect, the Islam that I learned and practiced in Pakistan and now in Canada; the Islam of the *Qur'an* and Prophet Muhammad that instilled respect for all humanity; that is a moral and ethical code and, above all, values justice. I also talked about my children who are caring, believing Canadian Muslims. Afterward, people asked me about diversity within Islam. I said there are various paths that lead to God–the same God of the Jews and Christians whom we call Allah.

One person asked me how difficult it is to practice Islam in Canada. I told her that as a Muslim woman I can practice my faith more easily in Canada than I can in many Muslim countries where extremism and a warped ideology have taken over the norms of respect and tolerance. I pointed out that I'm a Sunni married to a Shia and noted that my kids are fondly called "Sushis."

At the end of my presentation, a perturbed looking woman, a teacher, asked to speak to me privately. She explained that she has many Muslim students so she decided to learn about Islam by attending classes at a Toronto mosque.

"Everything they told me at the mosque is at odds with what you are saying here today... you talk about similarities between Muslims and "people of the book"; they said there is no point of reference for Muslims and non-Muslims. When I asked about the different sects–because my students are from diverse denominations–they said that Shias, Ismailis and Ahmedis are not Muslims. You talk about finding liberation and freedom as a woman within Islam, but at the mosque the women weren't even allowed to speak."

"You've blown my mind. Why isn't a narrative like yours being heard all over Canada?"

I replied that my views are those of the silent majority who unfortunately are just that–silent. But after the spiraling events of Madrid, Britain and now Ottawa, we can no longer remain silent. So, my concerns and my questions to the Canadian Muslim community are: Why is the narrative of extremism taking precedent over voices of sanity and sense? How is the culture of extremism being kept alive in Canada. What are we going to do about it?

Never in the history of the world as I know it has there been such extensive dissection, dialogue and discussion about a faith as there has been about Islam, post-September 11, 2001.

Muslims have been stripped naked by the likes of Christian fundamentalists Jerry Falwell and Pat Robertson and political interviewer Oriana Fallaci. Even some local Muslims made a name for themselves by pointing out the trouble with Islam.

In this atmosphere rampant with distrust and fear, people became confused. As a Muslim involved in doing damage control, it was time to go back to the books and read, which is the first message of the *Qur'an*. In the immediate aftermath of 9/11, many Muslim scholars and intellectuals spoke out. We were exposed to books and writings by leading edge thinkers such as Khaled Abou el Fadl, Dr. Abdul Aziz Sachedina and Canadian professor Amir Hussain. More importantly for me, women's voices were being heard, such as Amina Wadud.

It was prime time for interfaith outreach and the United Church of Canada took the lead in Muslim-Christian solidarity by working on a document called *That We May Know Each Other*. We started to build bridges of understanding and fellow Canadians realized that it's not about Islam and the West but Muslims in the West. These Muslims are under massive pressure since 9/11 and have faced a severe backlash. But other communities have reached out and vice-versa. Recently, when the Jewish community was victimized by hate-fuelled vandalism, Muslims stood by them and supported them in their cause. There was hope on the horizon.

> We must take back the mosques to ensure the voices of reasonable Muslim men and women are heard over the stringent calls for a physical jihad.

That hope is dashed every time a Muslim is allowed to indulge in hate propaganda and polemics. There is a problem when my university-going son asks why Muslim student associations spout venom against non-Muslims. There is cause for concern when anti-American rhetoric becomes the flavour of the month and justifies a different kind of polemic. All this has to stop. But how?

The Muslim Council of Britain has taken the unprecedented step of writing to every British mosque, urging people to help in the fight against terror. A Rand report published recently says that Americans must give precedent to progressive and moderate Muslim voices.

In Canada we have to do the same. But this effort must come from both sides. Officials dealing with terrorism have to ensure they have evidence and that due judicial processes are followed. They have to build alliances with Muslims and create credibility.

At the same time, it is imperative for Muslims to speak out against human rights violations and take urgent action to see that terrorism, extremism and anti-Western propaganda are eliminated.

In Canada, we must take back the mosques to ensure the voices of reasonable Muslim men and women are heard over the stringent calls for a physical jihad.

Our jihad is to ensure that Canada remains a safe and peaceful environment for Muslims and non-Muslims alike.

Reducing God to a Policeman
June 2003

Recently, I was invited by the Innoversity Summit to participate in a panel discussion on why Muslims are misrepresented by Western media. Next to me was a man, young enough to be my son, who made an excellent hi-tech presentation and at the end, when everyone was milling around, saying, "Good work," I held out my hand to congratulate him, as well. He pulled his hand back and said solemnly, with a straight face, "I don't shake hands with women."

To say I was shocked would be an understatement. Not only did I find his attitude disrespectful, I wanted to challenge him and ask why he was there; was he was afraid of women or his own sexuality? But I held my tongue because that would mean making a mockery out of Muslims, which is exactly what we were there to discuss.

As I fumed about this incident, someone kindly pointed out that certain restrictive misinterpretations of Islam condemn shaking hands with the opposite sex. I reminded them that people judging actions of Muslims without looking at the intention have a small view of moral and spiritual issues. Through our misinterpreted actions, we Muslims often create our own propaganda.

A few days later, I was giving a public address on Islam and women at a human rights event. A youth remarked that maybe my message would be more meaningful and have a better impact if I covered my head! At the risk of being told (which I have!) "You have amazing eye contact for a Muslim woman," I looked him straight in the eye and said, "Were you listening to the message or looking at the highlights in my hair?" It's this kind of monitoring, rampant in our faith, that makes me wonder about bickering over mundane petty issues that reduce the status of God to a mere policeman and move us away from the beautiful message of love, compassion, justice and truth.

> Through our misinterpreted actions, we Muslims often create our own propaganda.

I made the point of telling the young man distinctly that the injunction for modesty is for both men and women. However, since Muslim men have always interpreted Islamic shari'a law, they spend more time telling women how to be women, thus losing sight of the actual message. In this process, I gained some valuable insight on the controversial topic of interpretation, which continues to cause confusion amongst Muslims. A friend sent me an article by Holly Lebowitz Rossi from the Religion News Service called "Scholars say that the Battle for the Soul of Islam Neither Accurate nor Appropriate". In the article, the author quotes Sulayman Nyang, professor of African and Islamic Studies at Howard University in Washington D.C., who says we should be asking who controls the power of interpretation of the Muslim belief system or *din* in Arabic. "The battle is for what that *din* means....today," Nyang says.

Nyang is obviously referring to the emerging trend in some countries to enforce shari'a law, as we see happening in Pakistan today. Nyang states, "There is this contestation over who defines Islam and who can use his or her interpretation of Islam to justify the right of certain people to govern." This point resonates in my conscience as I watch the so called shari'a laws being used to specifically target women and suppress their human rights. In some cases, women interpret shari'a to their own detriment, as in the case of the Muslim woman in Florida who insists on getting her driving license without a photo and has sued the state court for wishing to implement the law. (Despite the fact that thousands of Muslim women drivers who wear hijab have their photos on their licenses.)

My interpretation of this case is simple. Follow the laws of the land or choose to live happily in a place like Saudi Arabia, where women aren't allowed to drive at all. That is the Saudis' interpretation of the shari'a, along with other misogynist and harsh injunctions over women.

Amina Wadud, professor of Islamic studies at the Commonwealth University in Virginia and author of *Qur'an and Woman,* is an excellent ambassador for women's rights in Islam. Recently, she presented a paper at an international conference on AIDS and HIV held by Prime Minister Mahatir Mohamad of Malaysia, who is one of the more progressive Islamic leaders. Twenty delegates stormed out after Wadud suggested that some Islamic teachings worsen the spread of the disease. Wadud faces the wrath of the extremist conservatives who accused her of blasphemy when she said, "Islam and Muslims exacerbate the spread of AIDS and...a traditional Islamic theological response can never cure AIDS."

She explained that Muslim women are bound by Islam to comply with their husband's desire for sex and can be punished if they do not. After being accused of demonizing Islam, Wadud told reporters that she stood by her comments. "My paper just states opinions that are different from others..." Difference of opinion has been the hallmark of Islamic jurisprudence with five accepted Muslim legal schools of thought, but the ability to accept a difference of opinion has been erased in present time.

Shari'a is a body of rules and regulations based on the *Qur'an* and Sunnah. To follow the shari'a means living a morally responsible life. It's ironic that shari'a, which means "the broad path leading to water" (the idea of water being fluid and flexible), has been made inflexible and rigid. It's the road of moral, ethical and just activity that all Muslims can follow wherever they live. Many Muslims practice shari'a while living under the Canadian Charter of Rights and Freedoms, which is not at odds with shari'a as it should be understood and practiced. It does not have to be forced as in Nigeria, Sudan and Pakistan, where assertion of shari'a is a political act, which reduces women and minorities to second-class citizens.

Al-Ghazzali (d. 505/1111), one of the most famous thinkers of his time, held that each Muslim must have enough knowledge of the shari'a to put it into practice in his or her own life. Nevertheless, other scholars have warned against too much time implementing shari'a since it can blind people to the other dimensions of the religion, which are also essential. Shari'a cannot exist without *ijtehad* (working out principles), *ijma* (consensus), *qiyas* (analogy), and most of *all-aqi* (reason).

Essentially, the laws of Islam must never be distorted to destroy the morality of Islam. Those who misuse and enforce laws in the name of Islam destroy the moral fabric of society. The president of Pakistan, Pervez Musharraf, has just warned residents of Pakistan against adopting the Taliban version of Islam in the country which is struggling for economic recovery and progress. "We are being called terrorists, fundamentalists, extremists and intolerant," Musharraf said. "We have to decide whether we need Talibanization or progressive Islam."

Order a Fatwa–Delivered in 30 Minutes or It's Free!

October 2003

A *fatwa* on moi? Last week I received a fatwa against an annual event that I host.

According to Khaled Abou El Fadl, law professor at the University of California, a fatwa is "a non-binding legal opinion issued in response to a legal problem."

This fatwa was for an event called Milaad, which features poetry or literature written in honour of the Prophet's birth, his life and achievements. Although this celebration is not an Islamic duty, it is a spiritual tradition developed by Muslims out of love and reverence for Prophet Mohammad and his family. I've celebrated and participated in Milaads since I was a child. In those days, there were no extremists hounding us.

I knew that sooner or later, some religious crank would find me but still I was surprised when I saw the email with my name on it. I'm no stranger to hostility... I've received pepper spray, crank calls and hate mail; my husband has been taken aside and asked why he "allows" his wife so much freedom to speak out; at various times people have suggested that I write under a pseudonym or change my name entirely; and my family lives in fear of my shooting from the hip, but I've never given any of this serious thought.

I give Canada credit for this honour. It's only when I came here 14 years ago that I found freedom and confidence as a Muslim woman to study and come to understand that my faith, Islam, does not bind me but frees me to pursue knowledge and strengthen my spirituality, regardless of my gender. In Canada, I've had the opportunity to meet and converse with progressive scholars like Dr. Azizah al Hibri, Dr. Abdulaziz Sachedina and Dr. Khaled Abou el Fadl, who helped me understand my faith with reason, appreciating its various nuances and diversities.

> I knew that, sooner or later, some religious crank would find me. I'm no stranger to hostility and my family lives in fear of my shooting from the hip.

The resulting liberation of my mind has allowed me to reflect upon and critique some of the false ideologies being promoted by my coreligionists, especially those who take direction from a deviation of Islam, which forms the state religion of Saudi Arabia, and makes a mockery of our faith. This obviously has not endeared me to many who want to cling to the illusion that they are the chosen ones, and their way is the only way.

Since long before September 11, I've been writing and speaking about issues that we, as Muslims are grappling with. I've spoken out about injustices against women and minorities, about gender equality, against intolerance and interfaith polemics, against extremism and violence of all kinds, including suicide bombing, and most often about inflexible interpretations of Islam that force all joy out of our traditions.

CHAPTER 1: CRISES OF ISLAM

Last year, just before I celebrated my annual Milaad, I found an article in an ethnic newspaper with a message from Shaykh Abdel Azeez al-Sheikh, Grand Mufti and highest religious official in Saudi Arabia. He blasted these celebrations as heresy and condemned them as "mimicking Christians." So, I promptly wrote an article in *The Toronto Star* and explained the history of the Milaad tradition, placing it at the time of the Prophet and explaining that it is a custom that was developed out of love for our Prophet. I thought I had made my point and could rest easy. But the policing does not stop. This year, my email invitation for Milaad made its way to an organization in America called the American Muslim Association of North America–the Islamic Center for Reaching and Preaching. Al-Amana boasts of a fatwa service. Fatwas by Al-Amana Shura advisors.

"We search before giving a fatwa," they proudly declare on their web site.

Wow. I'm impressed. Despite the countless people indulging in devious activities, they found little ole me to send their fatwa to. According to their long, boring, email (which is adapted from Majmoo Fatawa Samahat al-Shaykh Abdel Aziz ibn Baz), I've received ruling number 2/882.

What an enriching life these guys must lead. They even have a toll free number, 1-800-95-FATWA!

They should know that it will take more than a fatwa to deter me. So I had my celebration over the weekend. What better way to celebrate Thanksgiving than a thank you to God over samosas and tea, with my friends, family and well wishers, including men who came to show support.

If organizations like Al-Amana are allowed to exist freely in North America, then I would like to see fatwas issued against governments who allow:

- Subjugation of their entire female populous
- Killing of journalists
- Persecution of minorities
- Waging war against innocent men, women and children

American Muslim Convert Critiques Mosque Culture

April 2004

It has been two decades since academic and author Jeffrey Lang made the passage from atheist to devout Muslim, yet he remains as passionate as ever about his conversion.

Born to a Roman Catholic family in Bridgeport, Connecticut in 1954, Lang spent his early years questioning the existence of God and finding no satisfactory answers.

"I rebelled against all the institutions that society held sacred, including the Catholic Church," Lang said in a recent talk to Toronto's Forum for Learning, where he spoke from the heart about his passage from questioning to conviction and from bitterness to belief.

His abusive home life with an alcoholic father led to more bitterness, so at 16, Lang publicly declared himself an atheist. In 1982, at age 28, Lang accepted Islam, based primarily on a chance reading of the *Qur'an*.

As Lang became a practicing Muslim, he also experienced the challenges of being a convert, both from within and outside the community.

"It's lonely being a convert to Islam," he said in an interview following his address. "I felt vulnerable and disconnected from the host community and needed support.

"The Muslim community was somewhat critical that I wasn't conservative enough and that there was no physical change in my appearance...but I didn't become Muslim to enter into a community–I already had a family. I wanted to be accepted as I am and this was a challenge."

To address these challenges, Lang wrote *Struggling to Surrender–Some Impressions of an American Convert to Islam,* in which he also tackled the rigidity of the mosque culture.

"At first, I used to attend mosque for the five daily prayers and I loved going there, but once I got married and had girls, they were not welcome at the mosque," he wrote.

"I would like to see mosques being more family friendly. Presently they are like a men's club."

Lang has three daughters ages 17, 16 and 14. "Without me, my girls would lose their only link with Islam and I don't want that to happen." After his book was published, Lang received hundreds of e-mails, letters and phone calls.

"Mostly from atheists, converts and second-generation Muslims (living in the West) who also feel alienated from the mosque culture," he said. His latest book, *Losing My Religion: A Call for Help* is based on the feedback he received from second-generation Muslims.

It illustrates that Lang has grown increasingly concerned about the future of young Muslims in America. He says many do not feel welcome at the mosques and are falling away from the faith.

He suggests the mosque should be a place for spiritual education and bonding. "Cultural tradi-

Chapter 1: Crises of Islam

tions that are nonessential need to be removed. Mosques should not become a cultural asylum."

In the recently published book, Lang has offered solutions. "Take back the mosque," he says. "Don't give it up or smother Islam–that will keep our children away. Make it user-friendly, let women become an essential part of the mosque."

His wife is on the board of directors for their local mosque.

> "Many Muslims from around the world have expressed to me their hopes that the USA Muslim community will lead the way toward Islamic reform, but I keep responding that my hopes are in Canada."

After his talk in Toronto, as Lang was autographing books for his audience, a young man came up to him and said, "Dr. Lang you've made a believer of me. I was an atheist but now I want to revisit my faith."

Lang had a very positive experience in Canada and upon his return to Kansas, wrote to say, "Many Muslims from around the world have expressed to me their hopes that the U.S.A. Muslim community will lead the way toward Islamic reform, but I keep responding that my hopes are in Canada."

"This latest trip has left me all the more convinced that Canada is where to look for an Islamic reformation. "I only hope our community in the U.S. gets dragged along."

CHAPTER 2
IMAGES OF ISLAM

Understanding Jihad

There are five pillars of faith in Islam, which include belief in one God, fasting, prayer, going for the pilgrimage and giving charity. Some religious authorities claim a sixth pillar: *Jihad.* In the past decade, this word has become well known in English because of the contemporary world situation, which has made it the focus of media, which have very often used it out of context.

Interpreting the term jihad to mean "holy war" is misleading and usually inaccurate. The Qur'anic usage of the term jihad is much broader than the political use of term might imply. The basic meaning of jihad is "struggle" and this struggle is not necessarily an armed struggle. It can mean the struggle for truth and justice or good over evil.

When we understand the word Islam to mean "submission" or "surrender", then in a certain manner, jihad complements Islam. This surrender is not passive behavior, but takes place actively and willingly to God's command, since it is for God's will that people struggle in his path. Hence, submission demands struggle. In order to submit fully to God's commands, people need to be aware of all that is evil or negative around them and within themselves that pulls them away from God. Therefore, submission to God and struggle in his path go together hand-in-hand, and neither is complete without the other.

Within the Islamic context, the fact that submission to God demands struggle in his path is self-evident. The basic tenets of Islam, fasting, prayer and pilgrimage are all achieved through inner struggle. It takes a great deal of self control and struggle to submit to an unseen higher authority and also to deal with the pressure of society to conform.

The true meaning and place of jihad in a Muslim's life is illustrated through a well-known tradition of the Prophet Mohammad. When he had returned to Medina from a battle with the enemies of the new religion, he is quoted to have said, "We have returned from the lesser jihad to the greater jihad." The people asked, "O Messenger of God, what jihad could be greater than struggling against the unbelievers?" He replied, "Struggling against the enemy in your own breast."

Muslim scholars who claim that jihad is a sixth pillar of Islam usually refer to the fact that struggle in the path of God is a necessity for all Muslims. It is also recognized that this struggle will sometimes take the role of outward war against the enemies of Islam. The *Qur'an* also says that in some cases war becomes a contingency–especially as a means of self-defense. In chapter two of the *Qur'an*, it says: "war may become necessary only to stop evil from triumphing in a way that would corrupt the earth."

Chapter 2: Images of Islam

It needs to be stressed that war is only acceptable as a means of self-defense and to protect the faith. In times of war, stringent rules are applicable. The *Qur'an* says: "and slay not the life which Allah has made sacred, save in the course of justice." The Prophet of Islam told his companions and followers in the instance of the first war of Islam, when their lives were threatened and they had to revert to self-defense, that they could never harm innocent people, children, civilians, old people, people engaged in any worship or destroy crops and animals. The *Qur'an* says clearly: "only the combatants are to be fought and no more harm should be caused to them than they have caused." Thus wars and weapons of destruction that destroy civilians and their towns are totally ruled out by the *Qur'an* and by practice of the Prophet.

In current times, there is a huge debate taking place about the way terrorists interpret the *Qur'an* to justify jihad to mean violence. Karen Armstrong, in an article for The Guardian, entitled "Unholy Understanding of Holy Texts", writes that we distort our scriptures if we read them in an exclusively literal sense. She explains that all verses in the *Qur'an* are called "parables" (*ayat*) and its images of paradise, hell and the last judgment are also *ayat*–pointers to transcendent realities that we can only glimpse through signs and symbols. Armstrong clarifies that this is the reason Muslim extremists have given the jihad (which they interpret as "holy war") a centrality that it never had before and have thus redefined the meaning of Islam for many Muslims. She also says that in this they are often unwillingly aided by media, who also concentrate obsessively on the more aggressive verses of the *Qur'an*, without fully appreciating how these are qualified by the text as a whole.

Oklahoma, When Will the Violence Stop?

May 1995

As a mother I am shattered and my heart weeps for the parents of the children killed in Oklahoma. As a human being I am horrified and appalled about the tragic events in a peaceful city that is forced to focus on the ongoing discovery of dead bodies amidst the debris that was once an inhabited building.

I cannot begin to comprehend or accept that there are people living in the civilized world who will stoop to violent and barbaric attacks on innocent men, women and children. Right now, I ache for those who have lost family and friends in the bombing. If I hurt thousands of miles away, I wonder how the residents of Oklahoma feel. I don't think I can even begin to gauge the depth of their despair and grief.

For whatever its worth, I do share in their anguish. If the survivors of this recent and uncalled for hideous attack on civilians feel malice and outrage at the offenders, they have every right to do so. I also abhor and despise the attackers for their cowardly act, as millions of other people surely do, because acts of brutality against innocent human beings can never be justified.

Media and politicians are looking for suspects, reasons and motives. They have called out their experts in terrorism, in Middle East politics and criminologists. I feel, however, there is no reasoning behind terrorism. There is never a motive behind killing innocent people except a depraved mind. If they do find who executed the bombing and why they did it, will it lessen the agony of those affected? Of course I understand that an investigation has to be made, but in the meantime we cannot just stand by waiting for something to happen. We must extend our compassion and our heartfelt sympathy to those touched by this gruesome tragedy. It might help the people of Oklahoma and those around them to understand that most people, regardless of nationality, faith, culture or creed are with them in their time of crisis. We do not defend the motive or the criminals. Whether it is gas poisoning in Japan, suicide in Waco Texas, a bombing at the Trade Centre in New York or a pipe blast in Charlottetown, we are equally distressed by the incident. There is absolutely no place in civilized society for blatant acts of terrorism and we as nations, communities and also as individuals must openly condemn these acts and ensure ways to eradicate the diabolic evil that has infiltrated our society.

It has become the norm to tie in acts of terrorism with religious groups. Tell me which religion advocates killing of innocent people? Certainly not any faith with which I am familiar. And if there are people out there who commit ghastly crimes in the name of religion, then they need to be ousted from that religion because they are maligning the faith of others and putting it to test.

There is no excuse or provocation in any religion that condones senseless killing. In fact, most major

Chapter 2: Images of Islam

religions of the world condemn senseless acts of violence and are trying to propagate peace in the world. Those who do not adhere to policies of peace, love and goodwill towards all are obviously from a cult or fanatic organization that does not draw its mandate or strength from a religion. There is no place for such radicals in the pursuit of any faith and to accept such maniacs is to lead to eventual eradication of human values that we hold dear to us. Many of us came to North America to escape the influence of extremists who massacre, mutilate and destroy in the name of religion. Unfortunately, today religion is used as a crutch for many inhuman acts of depravity and this trend must be stopped.

If we are to live in a peace-loving society, then we must unanimously condemn terrorism and acts of brutality no matter who masterminds them. It is our right as free human beings and our responsibility to those around us to ensure the world remains free of slaughter and destruction. I realize that America at one time or the other has meddled in affairs of many countries resulting in bloodshed and the loss of millions of lives. Saddam Hussein living free today is an example of the terror America has unleashed on the Middle East. Saddam alone is responsible for the destruction of millions of innocent men, women and children. Today, the killing fields of Russia, Bosnia and Rwanda are marked with the

> Let us take a united stand and unanimously condemn all acts of terror in the past and the present and struggle together to create a peaceful future for our children.

blood of the innocent. However, that still does not justify the senseless bombing in Oklahoma. Violence cannot be fought with counter violence. It just makes the circle a never ending round of dead bodies–which does not achieve anything in the end.

Right now people in Oklahoma, Charlottetown and New York are living in fear of what will happen next and glancing at each other in suspicion. This is the legacy of terrorism and we want no part in it. We as human beings are saddened, devastated and shocked by all incidents of violence.

Let us take a united stand and unanimously condemn all acts of terror in the past and the present and struggle together to create a peaceful future for our children.

Their Jihad is NOT My Jihad

July 2002

Since September 11, 2001, I've been invited to many churches, schools and community centers to speak about Islam to non-Muslims. People curiously ask if I'm trying to convert others or get converted myself! I tell them it's neither: What I do is essentially "damage control".

With time, I thought this fleeting interest in Islam and Muslims would fade, like a passing fad. Much to my surprise, it hasn't and today, one year down the road, I still find myself doing the rounds, teaching Islam 101! One of the most satisfying aspects of these sessions is the Q & A's; this is when real issues surface and the spectre of an unknown fear is put to rest. I usually start off by telling my listeners that no question is too controversial and no issue too contentious for me. Questions have ranged from the sublime to the ridiculous: "How many wives does your husband have?" to "What is the history of the turban in Islam?"

However, there is one serious question that is posed every time, in various formats: "Is violence a part of your faith and does it say, somewhere in your scripture, that suicide is an honourable act to be rewarded by God? Is killing non-Muslims a form of jihad?"

It concerns me that while I spend valuable time and energy informing non-Muslims about the true interpretation of jihad (moral, intellectual and spiritual striving) and that violence and suicide are forbidden in Islam, there are many people in positions of authority within the Muslim world who simultaneously promote and condone violence. These are Islamists who believe their jihad is physical violence against civilians seen to be their enemy; to blow themselves up for political aims and to rid the earth of non-Muslims.

Obviously, their jihad and my jihad are not the same. I believe the jihad preached and practiced by the Messenger of Islam Mohammad is not the one being propagated by people who support the path of violence against civilians, or who encourage the destruction of lives through suicide bombings.

Muslims unanimously hold there is no greater example of conduct for us than the Prophet Mohammad. For the first twelve years of his mission, he actively pursued a policy of non-violence and arbitration. For the following ten years he participated in war only when he had to, but preferred mediation and non-violent confrontations. As well, during time of war, the Prophet imposed severe restrictions on his generals and armies about not harming civilians, the environment, places of worship, women or children. Adhering to the teachings of the Prophet, his family and followers also persevered in the tradition of non-violent peacekeeping. Hence, I tell my audience, throughout hundreds of years of the spread of Islam, there is no recorded history of suicide being used as a weapon.

Chapter 2: Images of Islam

There are heart-rending traditions of sacrifice and valour as Muslims faced far graver threats and challenges than they are up against today, but history records no exemplary acts of suicidal destruction. This is a relatively new phenomenon, not necessarily specific to the Islamic world. Japanese Kamikaze pilots; "suicidal" military exploits of the defenders of the Alamo and Tamil Tigers are other examples. The rise of suicide bombing amongst Muslims is unsettling because many Muslim clerics and scholars, well versed in the *Qur'an*, remain ominously silent when it comes to condemning suicide bombers and acts of terrorism against civilians. Suicide bombings challenge two fundamental principles of Islamic ethics: the prohibitions against suicide and the deliberate killing of noncombatants.

The *Qur'an* states clearly that killing one person is like killing all of humanity and taking your own life is a sin. Today, the Muslim world stays dangerously silent and from the same pulpits where hate is spewed comes the potent sanction of murderous missions. Young, impressionable Muslims, frustrated by their cause, are led to believe that suicide missions will take them straight to paradise. Some of these misguided youths are promised virgins in paradise as their reward. Keeping in mind these decrees are normally given by males, I call such promises wishful thinking!

While there is no doubt in my mind about the legitimacy of the Palestinian cause and the ongoing destruction of its people's lives and lands, there is still no parallel or justification for suicide bombings. Some argue that it is acceptable through the clause of reciprocity. But this thinking abrogates the moral and ethical teachings of Islam, which does not allow a people to stoop to the level of their enemies, but insists that Muslims must behave according to the tenets of their own faith, which gives clear and lucid guidelines.

Martyrdom is the will of God, not humans. It doesn't provide religious or political clout– in fact, it reduces the power of any just cause. Justice or "adl" is a key concept in the *Qur'an*. Justice is described as the avoidance of excess. There should be neither too much nor too little; hence, the use of scales as the emblems of justice. Lest anyone try to do too much or too little, the *Qur'an* points out that no human being can carry another's burden or attain anything without striving for it.

The dilemma faced by the Muslim world today is echoed in another valid query. Where do we draw our strength of conviction and who empowers us to speak out against extremist voices from the pulpit? My audience is usually amazed when I inform them that Islam gives each one of us the freedom to logically research and interpret the *Qur'an* with reason

Chapter 2: Images of Islam

and intellect. This understanding has recently brought the voices of many Muslim modernists to the forefront, rallying the message, "Forward with the *Qur'an*" and insisting on the importance of independent thought, both at the collective level (in the form of "ijma") and at the individual level (called "ijtehad"), as a means of freeing Muslim thought from the dead weight of outmoded traditionalism. I add my voice to theirs, as we unflinchingly condemn those cults that practice and promote their own form of Islam and jihad rooted in ignorance, rituals and dogma.

If I, a Muslim woman, could ever be empowered to pass a fatwa (religious decree), I would declare these cults outside the fold of Islam. Somebody should.

> Muslim modernists are rallying the message, *Forward with the Qur'an* by insisting on the importance of independent thought as a means of freeing Muslim thought from the dead weight of outmoded traditionalism.

Role of Media in Creating Peace

November 2002

Peace is a natural and inherent need of human beings, which prospers when there is harmony among friends, neighbors and strangers. Harmony is achieved through tolerance, communication and discourse and most of all, by upholding truth and justice.

A simple perspective is that peace is the absence of conflict. The UNESCO constitution makes note that since wars begin in the minds of men, it is in the minds of men that the defense of peace must be constructed.

> If media was concerned about peace, there would be cameras all around to record the dialogues of peace that are going on across North America.

Media fuels the upholding or wrecking of this peace. Media thrives on conflict. If media was as concerned about peace as we are, there would be cameras all around to record the dialogues of peace that are going on across North America by people and organizations that are trying to build bridges of understanding and tolerance.

It is a sad fact that the media would be more interested in reporting on a war rally than a peace forum.

There is far more coverage of conflicts than there is of peace. There is a reason for that: media is not a natural phenomenon. Newspapers, news and opinions don't occur naturally; they are made as a result of human will, history, social circumstances, institutions and the conventions of one's profession. Media is our biggest challenge in this century. It represents one of the most powerful institutions in a democratic society. Media plays a powerful and potent role in shaping attitudes and perceptions, in dictating ideas and molding policy. Gerald Levin, The CEO of Time-Warner says, "It's up to media to lead society and humanity in the pursuit of justice, equality and progress."

You may well ask how.

I believe the answer is simple. Democracy depends on a free press. We need unbiased information to live our lives in peace and media is a key provider of information, so it is critical that this coverage, whether print or electronic, be fair and balanced. Western media can do amazing things. It has the political liberty to present all sorts of notions, to provide eccentric, aberrant and sometimes incorrect views. There is frequently little accountability and much leverage.

Take the story of the Washington sniper who brutally and knowingly killed eight innocent people. Yet the media didn't call him a terrorist. Which is the way it should have been reported.

Media doesn't use the same tolerance and understanding when it comes to the Muslim community. In his insightful expose of how Western media deals with Islamic issues, Professor Edward Said, author of *Covering Islam*, explains that the media consists largely of profit-seeking corporations and therefore, quite understandably, has an interest in promoting some images over others.

Closer to home, Haroon Siddiqui of *The Toronto Star* wrote in a column that writers and editors are being dictated by media owners. He says there is huge gap between media and consumers that needs to be tightened. The role of media in peacemaking, or rather the lack of it, has never been more apparent than after September 11, 2001. U.S. media blew September 11 events out of proportion and sensationalized the negative aspects of this event.

Even on our side of the border, I had many calls post-September 11 from journalists, TV stations and radio hosts, looking for sensational stories, for drama about anger and revenge, about violence and discrimination. They were disappointed with me because I always reminded them that September 11, despite its tragic impact, was certainly not the most tragic event in the history of the world. Thousands of innocent civilians are dying needlessly every day in other parts of the world and receive little or no recognition by media.

Secondly, I pointed out, there were many peacemaking and bridge-building stories that have never been told.

But the media was looking for sensation–because news that is sensational, that shocks, is in the end, news that sells the publication. As a result, many peace-making events all over the world were sidelined. For example, nowhere in mainstream media did we read that in Europe, soon after September 11, 2001, there was a peace gathering of many multi-faith spiritual leaders from around the world who prayed for universal peace.

As the first anniversary of September 11 rolled around, North American media was once again in the business of sensationalizing the event. I say North America media with intention, because the same is not true across the Atlantic. I've traveled across the Atlantic a few times since September 11, 2001 and news changes faster than aircrafts change time zones. News in Europe is more balanced and definitely less abrasive than in North America. In countries outside North America, the September 11 anniversary was used to commemorate Afghan victims, Iraqi children of war, African casualties of Aids and thousands of other innocent deaths. This was not the case here at home. While on the one hand we say violence begets violence, media makes no effort to downplay their role in perpetuating violence.

One of most potent weapons used by media is the war of words. Violent and confrontational terminology is key propaganda. A sad example of media's role in creating havoc is the disgusting remark made by American Baptist pastor Reverend Jerry Falwell during an interview conducted by CBS's 60 Minutes on October 6, 2002. Falwell told reporter Bob Simon that he believed the Muslim who commits acts of violence in jihad does so with the approval of Mohammad. "I think Mohammad was a terrorist," Falwell said. "He... I read enough of the history of his life written by both Muslims and... and non-Muslims, that he was a... a violent man, a man of war."

The remark itself was rude and repulsive enough to have been ignored, but media picked it up and it was on the newswire within hours. Adding insult to injury, 60 Minutes decided to air the issue on the weekend, making a sensitive Muslim community even more defensive. Thanks to Western media's irresponsible use of jingo-ism instead of journalism, Muslims today have been made synonymous with terrorism, fundamentalism and militancy, whereas the same epithets do not apply to those rogue states and people who have been actually engaged in the killing of civilians far longer than terrorism became a buzz word in media. Obviously, peace falls off the table when one community is targeted by media. In an article titled Hidden Meanings in Western Media's Language of Discourse, Zafar Bangash, director of Crescent International, gives a pertinent example of the Afghan mujahedeen. Bangash says that when the Afghans were battling the Soviets, the Western press referred to them as "freedom fighters". Once the Soviet army was banished, the Afghans became guerrillas. Now they are rebels and outlaws.

Kashmiri freedom fighters are called militants or separatists even though their state is recognized by the UN as disputed territory. How can a people who are not part of a country be called separatists while they struggle to secure their rights?

There are numerous other examples of media's role in creating conflict rather than perpetuating peace. I don't wish to focus only on the negative, so in all fairness, I think I should give you a recent example of a piece of media coverage that does promote peace.

In *The Toronto Star* recently, there was beautiful story about a Hindu in India, who owns a mosque and hires a Muslim Imam to perform prayers. The story talks about living in harmony and understanding. Now here is a story that promotes peace-making efforts and it does have an impact because I had a call from two journalists today, asking if I would comment on the story.

I consider myself to be very tolerant and since I work in media, I do have an understanding of how things work. However, my patience also wears thin when media knowingly and consistently puts a barricade in the peace process by promoting images and stories that are biased, ignorant and one-sided.

Since society depends on media, change will only come when truth and justice become the landmarks of a great media. We need this in Canada, where peace-making has been a long standing tradition.

Jihad in the Newsroom

May 2003

In the post-9/11 America, Muslim-bashing has become the national pastime–which is fine to some extent if the Americans would only get their terminology correct. Although almost anyone who could correctly pronounce "al-Qaeda" became an authority overnight on Islam and Muslims, the self-declared experts and the media couldn't get most of the jargon right.

For example, in the U.S. news, Muslims were called Islamics or Mohammedans. Even a seasoned journalist like Walter Cronkite referred to us as Muslimites.

> One reporter got so confused that she reported a Muslim woman wearing a jihad!

One reporter got so confused between hijab (which is a head covering) and jihad (a struggle) that she reported a Muslim woman wearing a jihad!

In Canada, when the media bash Muslims, at least they get their wording correct. September 11, with all its bleakness, has certainly put Islam on the map and I must say Canadian media has moved ahead with integrity and honesty. Not 100 percent accuracy, but in all fairness, Islam is confusing for many Muslims as well.

I'm not just criticizing the media, but actually indulging in some constructive analysis to give examples and make some recommendations. I feel qualified to do this because I am in the unique position of being a Muslim journalist who is also a woman and who works on both sides of the fence.

I gained valuable experience and objective insight by default. Thirteen years ago, when I came to Canada, I didn't intend to become a writer of stories about Islam and Muslims. Unfortunately, at that time there was very little coverage of Islam. When there was any, it was largely distorted. I found the majority of images that the public saw were those reflecting oil or turmoil. The terminology associated with Muslims was inflammatory and seditious. Hence, the stories that surfaced were stereotypical and superficial.

A case in point: when the media reported on the Muslim festival of Eid–which is the largest celebration of Muslims the world over–the images were always of men in a mosque with their heads down and butts in the air. I mean no disrespect to the fact that the men were praying, but what about the women, the children, the henna and clothes, the diversity and the color that are all part of the wonderful time of Eid?

As a result of the Canadian media's half-hearted attempts to cover Islamic events, a balanced Muslim diversity or a strong Muslim identity never emerged. It is sad, considering Islam is a cultural heritage that spans over 1,400 years.

As a Muslim activist and feminist, I was especially appalled at the negative portrayal of Muslim women in media. I kept examining the women who were portrayed in the stories; they are not part of the mainstream Muslim world that I know of.

When Islamic conferences or meetings were covered, only the men were interviewed. Now, this may have been a problem with the Muslim community or a cultural issue, but the media wasn't doing much to change the status quo. So I took to heart what Nihad Awad of the Council on American/Islamic Relations says: "Before we criticize, we must educate."

In 1999, I put together a resource kit for media called Muslim Women and Media which listed professional Muslim women as contacts. This kit reflected results of a poll and quoted Muslim women, especially young Canadian Muslim women, saying they would like to be asked to comment upon mainstream issues like the environment, elections and education.

I tried to empower media to reflect Muslims in the mainstream, not just in ethnic or religious stories. There is a fine line between culture and faith. Every story that has a Muslim in it is not always an ethnic or faith-related story.

Recently, *The Toronto Star* carried a special section on cottage country. My cottage story would have been part of that, except that my editor cut it. The editor said my story lacked magical, mystical, ethnic content. I tried. Truly, I incorporated everything from my nose ring to henna, but for Pete's sake, how ethnic can a true blooded Canadian cottage story be? The whole point of my story was that South Asians are not cottage people!

Through this exercise of trying to separate myth and reality, culture and faith, I learned that it is imperative to create awareness, both in the newsroom as well as within the community. This is what I believe I do best.

Why is awareness needed in the newsroom? Because that is where the story begins, where the decisions are made. If there is no diversity in the newsroom, then the result is sloppy and half-hearted. For example, when the female genital mutilation story broke (which is clearly not part of the faith, but a cultural practice), I called to ask *The Globe and Mail* if there was diversity training within newsrooms to handle a sensitive issue. The response was that there is no need for diversity training.

The fact is the media is no longer dealing with Islam and the West–it's Islam and Muslims in the West. Recent statistics show that Eastern religions and especially Islam are the fastest growing faiths in Canada. The number of Muslims has doubled in past 10 years, so it is obviously a demographic necessity and practicality to know more about a people that are an integral part of the community.

Canada's House of Commons' standing committee on foreign affairs launched a study on Canada's Relations with the Countries of the Muslim World. The study says that fundamental to enhancing those relations is improving our collective understanding of Islam and its peoples. An important step forward is to see the Muslim world's remarkable but often overlooked diversity and history.

In the past, media had an excuse because when they needed to find a person in the Muslim community to comment on a current issue, there were only a handful of people on their roster. It was always the same Imam of the same mosque commenting on women's rights or the lack thereof. I think the media lapped it up because it made for sensational if inaccurate stories. But today, with over 600,000 Muslims living across Canada (more than 400,000 in Ontario) from over 60 countries around the world, the expectation is that media would be able to get sound bites for almost any topic from a very diverse group, something that would be reflective of the real world of Islam.

The challenge for reporters is the Muslim community's fear of media, a mistrust that is rightly earned. Being chewed up and spit out by Ontario current affairs television show host Michael Coren can create long-term ego damage. I've been there so I know it's not easy to open up to a reporter who may be uniformed or poorly prepared for the interview.

Understanding the level of mistrust, in 2000, I created a guide for the Canadian Muslim community on how to be proactive with media at various levels.

It is interesting that other minority communities have also faced similar issues. In 2001, I worked as a consultant with the Periodical Writers Association of Canada (PWAC) and organized four workshops across Canada, which discussed racial barriers for minority writers. The resulting report for PWAC, entitled "Challenging Racial Barriers in Journalism", cites examples from the aboriginal and black communities illustrating how they have encountered barriers with media.

One recommendation made by the journalists at these PWAC workshops was for media and the offended community to interact more. I've tried to facilitate such meetings, but I must admit that sometimes they backfire and become media bashing sessions, which do not help the cause. Fortunately, there have been positive developments: CTV has created a diversity round table and *The Toronto Star* has established a diversity section and editor.

There is no doubt the Muslim community needs to be more accessible and available. Let's look at some of the hottest stories dealing with Muslims and how they were reported. Before the American war on Iraq, there was 9/11. What a mess the media made of that. In the mad scramble to feed the public's need for information, it appeared the media interviewed anyone who knew where Afghanistan was on the map. Very few of the so-called experts on Islam had read the history and politics of the region, or knew much about the faith. Afghan women, who were front and centre in the war, were usually overlooked by reporters. Most journalists missed the true essence of the bravery, heroism and strength of these women.

What the mainstream media needs to do is check accuracy, do their homework and become more balanced. It's alright to criticize Muslims when they are involved in political acts of sabotage, but at the same time, it is imperative to give the cause and effect. A story with no history or background remains superficial and unfair to the community.

The New York Times and The Washington Post have recently shown examples of balanced editorials where both Muslims and non- Muslims are discussing the state of the Muslim world without calling names. It is refreshing and allows Muslims to acknowledge the villains in their midst, without becoming defensive.

It is important, therefore, to build bridges and partnerships and to invite communication and dialogue before an event occurs that requires input from diverse communities. The media needs to understand that faith and culture are two separate issues. Muslims, like every other group of people, are multilayered. They are involved in every aspect of community life. There are grey areas. Not all stories dealing with Muslims are faith-related.

Are Our Civil Liberties at Stake?

November 2003

Rights and liberties are issues close to Muslims' hearts and minds. Muslims today find themselves caught between a rock and a hard place: the rock being an ideology gone mad–the likes of Osama bin Laden and his mentors; the hard place being the powers that support puppet regimes.

Moderate Muslims like me who want to differentiate our faith from extremist Muslims' twisted ideologies are facing increasing resistance. Sadly, it is in the interest of imperialistic powers to keep the general population of the world confused so the average public views Muslims as terrorists.

Here is an anecdote: In New York's Central Park, a dog was attacking a small boy. A young man passing by rescued the boy. A New York Times reporter who was nearby saw the incident and was impressed. He approached the rescuer and said the headline next day would read, "Courageous New Yorker risks life to save child". The man said he was not from New York. The reporter said, "No problem, the headline will read: Valiant American makes daring move to save child". The man said he's not American but a visitor from Pakistan. The headlines in *The New York* Times the next day read: "Pakistani terrorist attacks dog–al-Qaeda links being investigated".

When I first heard this, it was as a joke. Alas, it's no longer funny, as this perception has become reality. The consensus is: if it looks like a duck, walks like a duck, talks like a duck–it must be Muslim! An excessive, overzealous security agenda since September 11 has made Muslims feel anxiety, fear, alienation, betrayal and disillusionment. In the hours after the events of 9/11, scattered hate and racist attitudes were directed at Muslim Canadians on the streets of our cities, in schoolyards and workplaces, from strangers and from vandals who attacked places of worship. Ironically, racism combined with total ignorance rose to the surface, which led to hoodlums burning a Hindu temple and an attack on a Sikh man from Phoenix.

Next came mass detentions of Arabs and Muslims–dozens here in Canada, thousands south of the border, incarcerated under a cloak of secrecy. Secret detentions, secret hearings, secret evidence, secret names, secret numbers of those arrested.

Canada's Bill C-36 followed and quickly became law, allowing, among other things, preventative detentions and forced testimony–abominations in a free society. While some argued, rightly, that the Anti-terrorism Act did not single out Arabs and Muslims and is directed at all Canadians, we Arabs and Muslims nevertheless felt the act targeted a specific community. We were not wrong.

Civil liberties and human rights are the bricks that build a society. Once we allow them to start crumbling and decaying, the damage never stops.

The Jewish community is not new to persecution and hate crimes and it was during tough times like the ones I've mentioned that our friends in faith stretched out a hand of support and assisted Canadian Muslims in dealing with hate crimes. I worked with B'nai Brith to counter some of the issues with which we were dealing.

In the months following 9/11, there were reported abuses by law enforcement, and Canadian Security Intelligence Service in particular, which seemed to cast too wide a net. While on this terrorist fishing expedition, CSIS conducted intrusive interrogations of innocent people and, most damaging, pressured ordinary Arab Canadians to act as spies and inform on their friends and colleagues.

Media did not help. Unqualified "experts" on Islam and Muslims gave ignorant and uninformed opinions as they tried to paint all Muslims with the terrorist brush. The stereotypes and racist overtones put forward by some in the mainstream media confirmed the permissibility of singling out Arabs and Muslims for suspicious treatment. The message was: they are guilty by association; suspect by nature of their ethnicity and religion; therefore, an acceptable object of hate.

There were heartrending incidents, like a Muslim boy in Western Ontario who was hung by his non-Muslim friends. Police cars circled certain Ontario mosques at all hours of the day and Muslim women in hijab were abused verbally and physically.

This is all in the past, but I believe the situation today is worse. The Toronto Police Department records a 66 percent increase in hate crimes. We are currently seeing our civil rights being trampled. Following September 11, 2001, the Government of Canada approved sweeping new powers for the Royal Canadian Mounted Police, allowing officers to search homes without warrants, and gain access to a wider range of personal information. The Immigration and Refugee Law was also given the provision that allowed them to detain people based on reasonable suspicion.

As a result of this unleashed power, 24 Pakistani students were arrested for the crime of misrepresenting themselves to Immigration and detained for being enrolled as students at the Ottawa Business College, which turned out to be a scam. If being an illegal immigrant is a crime, then hundreds more in Canada should be rounded up and hounded like these young Pakistanis, who were first held in a maximum security facility where they were physically and psychologically abused by other inmates and later removed to solitary confinement.

> The effect on our community is palpable. Even people like me, who have been eternal optimists, feel the cold creeping in.

The RCMP claimed they removed five truckloads of material from these destitute students. The material turned out to be 35 mattresses, hardly evidence leading to terrorists or weapons of mass destruction. Some tactics now in practice are violations of the Charter of Rights: individuals are told there are a number of unanswered questions concerning them and that they "ought to come in" but that RCMP officers won't speak to them if they bring their own lawyers. The effect on our community is palpable. Even people like me, who have been eternal optimists, feel the cold creeping in.

Recently, a Canadian television studio called to invite me on a panel discussion regarding the aftermath of September 11. The journalist wanted to discuss my position regarding the rights and freedoms of Muslims in Canada. I made my stance very clear. He said, "But if September 11 had taken place in your country, Pakistan, they would have massacred the criminals." I told him the reason many of us came to Canada is for freedom and democracy, which we don't find in many parts of the third world.

If we are denied those basic human rights as Canadian citizens, and if Canada can't protect us, then what is the point in living here as loyal Canadians? Like our Japanese-Canadian counterparts during World War II, we, too, have become victims of psychological internment.

I am troubled that these days, anyone with a Muslim name or a beard and brown skin is questioned at border crossings, airports and even in their own neighborhoods. After the 1995 Oklahoma bombing, were people ever stopped at an airport because their name was Timothy? I have two sons, aged 18 and 20. They grew up here and are as Canadian as the goose or moose. They are unaware of the politics of power and are innocent bystanders. However, my husband and I have stopped them from traveling to the U.S. for the time being, until things blow over.

A member of parliament visiting from the United Kingdom remarked that he noted no mention of the civil rights issues regarding the 24 Pakistanis in any of the major newspapers. It is a shame for sure.

Do Muslims Eat Ketchup?

November 2003

In the course of my interfaith outreach, I've been asked many leading questions, including, "Who is a Muslim?" and "Do Muslims eat ketchup?" The short answer to the first question is: a Muslim is a person who shovels the snow off his neighbor's driveway and yes, we love ketchup and tomatoes, provided you're not throwing them at us.

> A Muslim is a person who shovels the snow off his neighbour's driveway and yes, we love ketchup and tomatoes, provided you're not throwing them at us.

More frequently, people ask me why I do this work. I found the answer in an article by Karen Armstrong, theologian and prolific author. She says,

> Every time a violent action or an intolerant word is spoken, the world becomes a worse place and the virus of evil and hatred spreads. But every time any single believer reaches out to others in compassion and sympathy, the world improves a bit.

This is what I believe my purpose is–to reach out and communicate that we have much to share in our heritage and traditions, provided we take time to understand each other.

My multi-faith perspective began at a young age. I studied in a convent and learned the Lord's Prayer before I learned my own Muslim prayers. It doesn't seem to have damaged my psyche.

I'm here to do damage control and correct some common fallacies about Islam and Muslims. This dialogue comes at a significant time for Canadians, when Eastern religions, Buddhism, Hinduism and Islam, are the fastest growing religions in the country, with the number of Muslims having doubled in the last decade.

Islam is the faith of 1.3 billion followers worldwide, one in every five human beings. Nearly four million Muslims live in North America. The Western media make it obvious that a better understanding of Islam is warranted. Whatever you do, please don't learn your Islam from CNN. From Samarkand to Spain and beyond, Islamic civilizations have produced great works of science, art, geography, medicine and philosophy, which, in turn, have made vital contributions to Western culture. These Muslim societies included sizeable and prosperous populations of Buddhists, Christians, Hindus, Jews and Zoroastrians–proof of the inclusive character of Islamic civilizations.

Therefore, the so-called Muslim world is not monolithic. With more than 182 million Muslims, Indonesia has the world's largest Muslim population, followed by Pakistan, India, Bangladesh and Turkey. Nonetheless, history and geopolitics (reinforced by recent crises) have often led Western observers to equate the Muslim world solely with the Arab world or the Middle East. All Arabs are not Muslim and all Muslims are not Arab. As a matter of fact, there are also Arab Christians and Arab Jews.

Chapter 2: Images of Islam

From Albania to Zanzibar, Muslims come from a tremendous diversity of backgrounds and speak a variety of languages, including Bengali, Chinese, Swahili, Persian, Turkish and English.

Recent global events have been framed as a clash of civilizations between the Muslim world and the Judeo-Christian West. This thesis is constructed on a faulty premise, one that sees Islam and the West as somehow having developed in isolation. To talk about such a clash is to make the fundamental mistake of forgetting the common basis of Western and Muslim civilizations.

Russell Baker, a New York Times journalist, points out that North America no longer boasts only a Judeo-Christian majority. North Americans should now be correctly referred to as people following a Judeo-Christian-Islamic tradition.

Two recent meetings in Washington, one hosted by Muslims and the other by a Jewish congregation, illustrate the heightened interest in exploring theological issues together. More than 700 people assembled in the sanctuary of Washington Hebrew Congregation, the area's largest Reform congregation, for a lecture by author Bruce Feiler on his book, *Abraham: a Journey to the Heart of Three Faiths*.

The gathering was the first of 100 interfaith Abraham Summits planned in communities across the country in connection with the book's publication. The book examines the man revered by Jews, Christians and Muslims as the father of monotheism. "At the heart of his story is unity," Feiler told the audience.

"At this time in history, it's either brotherhood or other-hood," he said. Differences in how the three faiths interpret God's message is natural, Feiler noted, drawing laughs as he commented, "As the father of four children, I don't see any contradiction in making one promise to one child and another promise to another child."

In the *Qur'an*, Jews and Christians are referred to as ahl al kitaab or people of the book. The *Qur'an* says, "Muhammad is but a messenger, before whom other messengers were sent", so Muslims are instructed to appeal to the people of book through what is common between them and Islam. Another verse in the *Qur'an* says,

> *Say o people of the book–come to common terms as between us and you: that we have to worship none but God, that we associate no partners with him, that we erect not from among ourselves Lords and patrons other than God. (HQ 3:64)*

So, instead of enhancing our differences, we can concentrate on strengthening our common goals.

The *Qur'an* tells us that our challenge is not to eliminate or hide differences but to live with them. Unity of human beings does not mean their uniformity. The *Qur'an* says, "O people we have formed you into nations and tribes so that you may know one another–not to conquer, convert, subjugate, revile or slaughter but to reach out with intelligence and understanding." In Islam, we address God as Allah in our prayers, which is an Arabic word directly translating into God with no gender specification. But we are also asked to reach out to God through 99 divine attributes or names. Most of these attributes reflect God's love, compassion and mercy for His people. The best way to experience the love of God is to love His creatures.

The understanding is that if we wish for God to be compassionate and merciful towards us, we must show the same compassion, mercy and respect towards His creation, which is all of humanity, the environment and animals. This compassion can't be selective for just a chosen few; it has to be for all.

The more we reach out to other human beings, the more we become a receiver and transmitter of God's radiance. In this way, we are drawn towards the source of all light–God, the almighty.

As an example of social justice and ethical values, Islam, like other Abrahamic religions before it, teaches us that God is just and the implementation of justice is part of God's purpose for human societies. As Muslims, we are charged with the duty of leading moral and upright lives. We are instructed not only to love one another, but to share the pain of our fellow citizens on earth.

Islam is a continuation of the Abrahamic tradition traced through Abraham's son, Ismail (Ishmael). It is the youngest of the three monotheistic faiths. Muslims believe the reason that Mohammad asked Muslims to pray towards Mecca, when they used to pray towards the Dome of the Rock in Jerusalem, was to draw people back to the spirit of Abraham, who lived before the arrival of the Torah and the Gospel and built the Kaaba as the first sanctuary to one God, not for any established religion.

The *Qur'an* reminds us to respect people of other faiths. God states clearly in the *Qur'an*:

> *Have faith in God and in that which has been sent down on Abraham, Ishmael, Isaac and Jacob and the tribes and that which was given to Moses and Jesus and the Prophets by their Lord. We make no distinction among any of them and to Him we have submitted. (HQ 2:136)*

Pope John Paul II said, while speaking to young Muslims in Morocco,

> Christians and Muslims have many things in common as believers and as human beings. We live in the same world, marked by many signs of hope, but also by multiple signs of anguish. For us, Abraham is a model of faith in God, of submission to His will and of confidence in his goodness. We believe in the same God, the one God, the living God, the God who created the world and brings His creatures to perfection.

It often surprises Christians that Jesus is mentioned more times by name in the *Qur'an* than the Prophet Mohammad. The *Qur'an* contains an entire chapter named Mary, regarding the birth of Jesus.

The *Qur'an* says, "lakum dinakum walayadin" (to you, your faith and to me, mine). It is a recorded tradition that a man came to the messenger of God, Mohammad, and said, "I have accepted Islam but my sons still follow the Christian faith. Please empower them to convert. Mohammad told him not to force his sons to change their faith. He recited, "La Ikra fi deen (there is no compulsion in religion), which was a message sent to Mohammad by God through the angel Gabriel, with the understanding

CHAPTER 2: IMAGES OF ISLAM

that God knows what is in people's hearts and is the implementer of justice and mercy. Sadly, some people breach the right to define the parameters of divine justice, and inflict satanic destruction on human society in the name of the faith.

Religion, like any other human activity, can and has been abused to denigrate and even persecute others.

The *Qur'an* says, "and slay not the life which Allah has made sacred, save in the course of justice." This means that killing one person is like killing all of humanity.

In the same essence, suicide is not permissible in Islam under any circumstance because Muslims believe God gives life and takes life. Truth and justice are two key themes in the *Qur'an*. In chapter 10, we read that,

God never considers it permissible to act unjustly towards his creation–it is rather people who render oppression and injustice. (HQ 10:44)

Islam teaches us to differentiate between right and wrong, between good and evil. There is a verse in the *Qur'an* (9:67), which translates, "enjoin the good and condemn that which is evil". This cautions us that, while we condemn the act, we should not condemn the person committing it. In other words, "Hate the sin but not the sinner."

There are no grey areas in our understanding of the difference between justice and injustice, combatant and non-combatant, legitimate and illegitimate use of force. As Muslims, we have been given very clear parameters.

The *Qur'an* says, that the Islamic relationship between individuals and nations is one of peace. Muslims learn from the *Qur'an* that God's objective in creating the human race in different communities was so that they could relate to each other peacefully.

Having said this, it is important to mention that the *Qur'an* also talks about war as a contingency. When the *Qur'an* was revealed, warfare was a way of life and desperate business in the Arabian Peninsula. A chieftain was not expected to spare survivors after a battle. In the *Qur'an*, the only permissible war is one of self-defense. Muslims may not begin hostilities.

War is always considered evil, but sometimes a war becomes the only solution to persecution and oppression.

There were strict guidelines to war. The Prophet told his companions that they could not harm civilians, old people, children or people engaged in worship, nor could they destroy crops or animals. Life and property of all, Muslim and non-Muslim, are sacred. The Prophet said, "Truly your blood, your property and your honour are inviolable."

The *Qur'an* says,

> *God commands men to act with justice and virtue and enjoins upon them generosity to kinsfolk. He forbids them evil deeds and oppression He admonishes you out of His mercy, so that you may accept His advice. (HQ 16:90)*

The understanding is that Islam rejects certain individuals or nations being favored because of their wealth, power or race. God created human beings as equal who are to be distinguished from each other, only based on their faith and piety. The Prophet Mohammad said:

> O People your God is one and your forefather Adam is one. An Arab is not better than a non-Arab, and a non-Arab is not better than an Arab; and a white person is not better than a black person and a black person is not better than a white person–except in piety.[25]

Islam teaches us that we should be just, even with those whom we hate, as God says,

and let not the hatred of others make you avoid justice. Be just: that is nearer to piety. (HQ 5:8)

The burning question is: What has so galvanized the violent tendencies in Islam that the faith has been transformed from a religion of love to a culture of hate? The answer is very complex. It is rooted in social, political and theological issues.

Stephen Schwartz writes:

> Throughout History, political extremists of all faiths have willingly given up their lives simply in the belief that by doing so, whether in bombings or in other forms of terror, they would change the course of history, or at least win an advantage for their cause.[26]

Karen Armstrong writes:

> Every fundamentalist movement I have studied in Judaism, Christianity and Islam is convinced

---

[25] Narrated in Mosnad Ahmad, #22978
[26] Schwartz, "Terrorism Has a Name - Wahhabism."

that liberal, secular society is determined to wipe out religion.[27]

She continues to analyze that fighting, as they imagine, a battle for survival, fundamentalists often feel justified in ignoring the more compassionate principles of their faith.

The theologically based attitudes of these absolute puritans are at odds, not only with a Western way of life, but also with the very idea of an international society or the notion of universal human values. In amplifying the more aggressive passages that exist in all of our scriptures, the religious extremists distort the tradition and implement hardships and restrictions on women, which are not in any way or form part of the faith.

At the time of the revelation, Islam came as a savior for women who were sold as slaves or buried alive in Arabia. Islamic injunctions gave women freedom, equality, the right to vote, own property, do business and not be obligated to hand over their earnings. They were also given freedom of choice in marriage and divorce. Unfortunately, there has remained a huge gap in the preaching and practice of Islam in the sphere of women's issues.

In Islam, there is no formalized priesthood, so the *Qur'an* is open to individual interpretation. There are religious scholars, called ulema, who are experts in the scripture, so Muslims are advised to choose an Imam or leader from amongst them, based on their piety and expertise in both secular and scriptural subjects.

---

[27] Armstrong, "Fundamentalism and the Secular Society."

Arabic is a rich and diverse language in which one word can have ten meanings or interpretations and needs to be understood in proper historical context and supported by practice and tradition of the Prophet, called Sunnah.

The ability of human beings to interpret texts is both a blessing and a burden. It is a blessing because it provides us with the flexibility to adapt texts to changing circumstances. It is a burden because the reader must take responsibility for the normative values he or she brings to the text. Any text provides possibilities for meaning, not inevitabilities. Those possibilities can be exploited or developed by the reader's good faith. In other words, the meaning of the text is only as moral as the reader. Misguidance is a universal phenomenon found in the outside world and within ourselves. Linking terrorism to Islam is like linking Pearl Harbor to Buddhism, Timothy McVeigh to Christianity or calling Baruch Goldstein, who shot 29 worshippers in the Hebron mosque, a true martyr of Israel.

Similarly, guidance is also a universal phenomenon. In other words, the human race is not conceivable without both prophets and devils. This leaves most of us between a rock and hard place. While we condemn acts of terrorism and sympathize with the victims, we find war against innocent civilians is not the solution to any problem.

War is a state of mind well-echoed in the UNESCO constitution, which notes,

> Since wars begin in the minds of men, it is in the minds of men that the defense of peace must be constructed.

In his message for the World Day of Peace on January 1, 2002, Pope John Paul II said, "No peace without justice, no justice without forgiveness."

This is the message of the ancient prophets and the bedrock of every true religion and true morality. The Prophet of Islam always looked for ways to eradicate injustice and inequity, looking upon them as the root cause of most evils.

The Pope went on to say that all world religions must cooperate to eliminate the social and cultural causes of terrorism by teaching the greatness and dignity of the human person and by spreading a clearer sense of the openness of the human family.

As an ancient poet once expressed it:

If there is light in the soul,
    there will be beauty in the person.
If there is beauty in the person,
    there will be harmony in the house.
If there is harmony in the house,
    there will be order in the nation.
If there is order in the nation,
    there will be peace in the world.

CHAPTER 3
TRUTHS OF ISLAM

Need for Compassion and Tolerance

Sept 30, 2001

In the name of God, the most gracious, most merciful
Praise to God, the cherisher and sustainer of the worlds
Most gracious, most merciful
Master of the of judgment
It is you we worship,
It is you we ask for help
Show us the straight way
The way of those on whom you have bestowed your grace–
   those whose position is not wrath and those who do not
   go astray (HQ 1:2)

This verse from the *Qur'an* is called the heart of the *Qur'an*. Many scholars believe that it encapsulates the entire spirit and essence of the holy book. It has also been likened to the Christian Lord's Prayer. We, as Muslims, recite this verse many times a day as we offer our five formal daily prayers and this prayer is a guide for us. We begin by praising God and calling Him merciful and compassionate.

The understanding is that if we wish for God to be compassionate and merciful towards us, we must show the same compassion and mercy towards His creation–which is the people around us. This may sound like a cliché but I always explain that I respect those who are my brothers and sisters in faith and I embrace those who are my equals in creation.

The *Qur'an* emphasizes the importance of human beings' vital relationships with God, his parents or the people around him in many verses. The Ten Commandments that Allah revealed to prophets Moses and Jesus constitute a complete guide that ensures the stability and safety of both the individual and society. Islam places great importance on social justice and ethical values.

> If we take this in context of the tragic events of September 11, we must understand very clearly and without a shred of doubt that the people who perpetrated this ghastly crime were not people of God.

We pray about mercy and accept that life and death are only in the hands of God. The *Qur'an* says: "and slay not the life which Allah has made sacred, save in the course of justice." God wants us to respect human life, telling us that killing one person is like killing all of humanity. If we take this in context of the tragic events of September 11, which left thousands dead, hundreds physically injured and the rest of the world spiritually wounded, we must understand very clearly and without a shred of doubt that the people who perpetrated this ghastly crime were not people of God.

They were those who went astray and if they used the name of Islam for the acts they committed, then they hijacked our faith. There is a verse in the *Qur'an* that translates: enjoin the good and condemn that which is evil or bad.

We, as practicing Muslims, totally condemn any action of violence against innocent people. Islam teaches us to differentiate between right and wrong, between good and evil, between justice and injustice, between combatant and non-combatant, between legitimate and illegitimate use of force. There are no grey areas in our understanding of these terms. As Muslims, we have been given very clear parameters between what is right and wrong. The *Qur'an* says,

The Islamic relationship between individuals and nations is one of peace. Muslims learn from the *Qur'an* that that God's objective in creating the human race in different communities was so that they could relate to each other peacefully.

However, the *Qur'an* also says that in some cases war becomes a contingency, especially as a means of self-defense. But even in such a case, there are extremely stringent rules of war. The Prophet of Islam told his companions and followers in the instance of the first war of Islam, when their lives were threatened and they had to revert to self-defense, that they could never harm innocent people, children, civilians, old people, people engaged in any worship or destroy crops and animals.

The *Qur'an* says,

> *Only the combatants are to be fought and no more harm should be caused to them then they have caused. (HQ 2:194)*

Thus wars and weapons of destruction that destroy civilians and their towns are totally ruled out by the *Qur'an* and by practice of the Prophet. This brings us to the very interesting and unending debate about the word jihad–misused and misrepresented by a few wrongly guided people.

It's very clear in the *Qur'an* that there is no such thing as Holy war. In actual fact, fighting a global battle against terrorism becomes by default our jihad in the true sense because jihad means struggle of good over evil. The *Qur'an* says further:

> *War may become necessary only to stop evil from triumphing in a way that would corrupt the earth. (HQ 2:251)*

So what else is terrorism but evil? In accordance with our Islamic mandate, we can't let it triumph. Terrorism is an attack against innocent civilians irrespective of their faith; terrorism is murder and genocide; terrorism is inherently evil no matter where it's generated from. The analogy of terrorism is like that of cancer; it's a disease that needs to be rooted out from the base and its connected cells need to be destroyed, otherwise it will raise its ugly head again and again.

So let us try and bring some order into this disorderly mess through our faith communities. Our faith tells us that in every time of darkness, there is some light. It's unfortunate that it had to take a catastrophe like 9/11 to bring us together, but we should continue to pray together and we should try and empower others to turn to prayer.

This is our only salvation. Let's pray for those who need it. Let's accept our emotions without letting them disable our clarity. Let's resolve to do what we can in our own humble way to help create a world of understanding, compassion, courage and most of all, love.

Jesus in Islam

October 2001

Islam, the faith of 1.3 billion people across the globe today, is a continuation of the tradition of Abraham, therefore embracing the two traditions preceding it, Judaism and Christianity.

Moses and Jesus preceded Mohammad as prophets and messengers, bringing the message considered to be the word of God and recorded in the *Torah*, the *Bible* and then the Muslim's *Qur'an*. Therefore, Muslims look upon Jews and Christians as "people of the book."

In Islam, we revere Jesus as a prophet, whom Muslims believe was unique among anyone who has ever lived or will live. Jesus is privileged by being given characteristics of healing, in such a way that was never precedented or repeated. Jesus is proof of the existence of God and His great mercies to mankind.

> Jesus and his teachings are mentioned more times in the *Qur'an*, than Mohammad.

The word Muslim means to "submit" to God. We believe that Jesus submitted to God in the most complete way through his compassion, justice and mercy for others. It's interesting that Jesus and his teachings are mentioned more times in the *Qur'an*, than Mohammad.

The references to Jesus in the *Qur'an* start with Mary. There is an entire chapter devoted to the birth of Jesus in the chapter titled Maryam (Mary). In this, God tells us about Jesus and his mother to inform us about his mortal and human nature.

> *Christ, son of Mary, was a messenger like many of the messengers that passed before him. His mother was a woman of truth. (HQ 5:75)*

Jesus performed miracles by God's permission just as God empowered Moses and several other prophets with miracles. God elevated their spirituality and humanity.

The *Qur'an* says that Mary was a faithful believer in God and asked God to protect her from Satan:

> *And her Lord accepted her with full acceptance and vouchsafed to her a goodly growth–prepared the conditions for that upbringing–and made Zachariah her guardian. [And the angels said], O Mary Lo God gives thee glad tidings of a word– and God's word is His will–from him whose name is Messiah, Jesus, son of Mary, illustrious in the world and the Hereafter, and one of those brought near to God. (HQ 3:45)*

It was said that Jesus would speak to mankind in his cradle–a miracle to prove the falsehoods of all the accusations concerning that Mary had a child– and he would be one of the righteous. Jesus said:

> *I am indeed a servant of Allah: He hath given me revelation and made me a prophet; And He hath made me blessed wherever I be and hath enjoined on me prayer and charity as long as I live; (He) hath made me kind to my mother and not over-*

bearing or miserable; So peace is on me the day I was born the day that I die and the day that I shall be raised up to life (again)! (HQ 19:15)

Regarding Jesus, the *Qur'an* says,

And he will teach him the scripture (the theory) and the wisdom to learn how to put it into practice), and the Torah and the Gospel. And will make him a messenger unto the children of Israel. (HQ 3:49)

It is believed that Jesus explained he had a sign from God, a sign that had to do with healing in a way that was miraculous and had to do with his relationship to God directly and not dependent upon human abilities. Jesus said,

I fashion for you out of clay the likeness of a bird, and I breathe into it and it be a bird, by God (it is God that gives it life). I heal him who was born blind, and the leper, and I raise the dead, by God's leave. And I announce unto you what ye store in your houses. Lo, herein verily is a portent for you, if ye are believers. (HQ 3:49)

The *Qur'an* goes on to say,

Lo, the likeness of Jesus is as the likeness of Adam (both were created without a father). He created him of dust, then He said unto him, Be! And he is. (HQ 18:59)

Muslims do not believe in the Trinity and have Jesus quoted as saying, "Lo I am a human being, not a God. Allah is my Lord and your Lord so worship Him. That is the straight path."

When Jesus became conscious of the disbelief of people about his prophet-hood, he cried, "Who will be my helpers in the cause of God?" The disciples said, "We will be God's helpers. We believe in God and bare thou witness that we surrendered unto Him."

And then God said,

O Jesus, Lo I am gathering thee and causing thee to ascend unto Me, and am cleansing thee of those who disbelieve and am setting those who follow thee above those who disbelieve until the day of Resurrection. Then unto Me ye will (all) return and I shall judge between you as to that wherein ye used to differ. (HQ 18:55)

Pursuing Peace through Education and Knowledge

March 2002

At a point in the history of the world, when religious intolerance is at an all time high, it's rare and refreshing to find a religious scholar who actively and consistently promotes peace and harmony. Dr. Abdulaziz Sachedina cherishes inclusiveness of all faiths. He says,

> The more I study other faiths, new traditions and various schools of thought, the more I understand my own faith.

Professor of Religious Studies at University of Virginia, he is a recognized expert in Islamic theology, law and ethics in the U.S. He sits with the U.S. congress and senate on a range of issues from cloning to biological research and is available to give advice on Muslim matters such as dietary laws in prison to wearing a beard in the police force. Apart from academia, Sachedina is an icon among Muslims of North America for his work in bringing the community together.

Sachedina's love for learning and imparting knowledge stems from his childhood. Born in Tanzania where he completed high school in Dar-es-Salaam, he says,

> Although my father died when I was 12, I recall growing up in an atmosphere that was

scholarly and intellectual, where reading was a tradition. I was drawn to a study of religion, and had a penchant for teaching and lecturing at a young age.

Influenced strongly by his mother, Sachedina says,

> My mother was a teacher, public speaker and advocate for women's rights and following her footsteps, I taught math, English and religion at age 13 to children younger than I.

Well on his way to becoming the powerful orator he is now, at age 17 Sachedina had his first experience in public speaking when he addressed over a thousand people about the Prophet of Islam and his teachings. He was a confident young man–too confident, he explains.

> Along with the religious influences I also inherited certain unhelpful attitudes–a defensiveness and narrow view of human religiosity so I used to argue about religion constantly when I was a youth.

All this changed in 1967 when Sachedina went to Iran to obtain his B.A. Honors in Persian language and literature. In Iran, he also took private lessons to learn Arabic and Islamic Sciences, including law, jurisprudence, theology, tradition and history.

> One of the greatest influences in my life and work is that of my teacher, Dr. Ali Shari'ati, well-known sociologist, historian and philosopher. Dr. Shari'ati saw history as an instrument of recording human experience as it goes through self-development and my analysis of history is influenced by his teachings. Dr. Shari'ati taught us to look at history as a whole, about inclusiveness and how to

strengthen religious knowledge without sectarianism.

Commenting on religious violence, Sachedina laments,

> I'm extremely saddened by people fighting in the name of religion. We can't use history to relive our differences. We need to use history to move on and resolve those differences through dialogue–not to make the same mistakes. And dialogue is between equals. We have no right to control the showering of divine mercy on humanity.

Sachedina's immense passion for peace shows on the contours of his face and the sadness in his eyes when he talks about sectarian violence.

> Religion becomes a weakness when used for violence by self-righteous and ignorant people and ignorance can only be erased through reading and reflection.

In his fervent pursuit of peace and understanding between communities, Sachedina cites a quotation from the *Qur'an* which he used as an introduction to a recent series of lectures.

> ...and had God not checked the evil oppressors among the people... a great number of monasteries, churches, synagogues and mosques where God's names is mentioned frequently would have been by now destroyed.

Attended largely by Muslim youth and non-Muslims, the purpose of these lectures was to remove barriers and bring people together. Sachedina moves easily from Arabic to Persian and back to

English, equally comfortable in Swahili, Gujrati, Urdu, Hindi, French or German.

Author of numerous books and papers, Sachedina, 58, has a soft spot for Toronto. "I share a special connection with Toronto for many reasons," he says. He proves this by coming to Toronto whenever he can, to share his knowledge and findings. From 1971 to 1976, Sachedina was a student at the University of Toronto where he completed his Master's degree and Ph.D. in Islamic and Middle Eastern Studies.

> Toronto was my first stint at studying Islam in the West and it was an eye opener. My teachers constantly challenged me to look in from the outside. I had already studied Islam from a religious perspective but Toronto was an opportunity to study Islam from a historical and intellectual perspective, a methodology which forced me to be objective.

He smiles as he recalls,

> When I presented my first dissertation proposal, my professor threw it back at me calling it defensive and subjective. Fact is, I was defensive about my faith and I'm grateful to my professors who forced me to weigh the strengths and weaknesses of my own belief system, as an outsider.

Sachedina doesn't downplay the effort his U of T professors to take him through this journey without hurting his faith.

> It was a transition from believer to observer and it helped me see the beauty of Islam as an outsider. Contours and landscape are always sharper and more attractive from a distance.

Sachedina's first job in 1976 was teaching Islam in Ontario at the University of Waterloo and Wilfred Laurier University.

> This was a time when Islamic history was a relative stranger to North American culture. It was considered history of "the other." The approach was patronizing and the methodology, orientalist, but thanks to my professors, I was prepared for the challenges.

In forty years of teaching at various academic institutions all over the world and lecturing his own community, Sachedina stresses the importance of reading and research.

> Our community in general is not a reading community. We tend to read only that with which we agree and have a comfort level, not anything that makes us think. This is detrimental to religion.

The Muslim community, which like many others, is victim of sectarianism, is not wholly comfortable with Sachedina's push for unity and minimizing differences. And Sachedina has been hurt by the implications.

> The community has difficulty choosing between academic language and the emotional rhetoric of the mosque. But I am an academic and have a responsibility towards history and to the community. In Islam, there is freedom to develop scholarship freely and this means that there is something to be learned from all scholarly works–irrespective of faith or sectarian leanings.

Do the challenges ever deter him?

> I believe in the power of divine guidance. When you enjoy what you do, you find a spiritual reward. I'm exhilarated when I read books, learn something new, or write a paper and I believe that from the Islamic perspective, if I stay within the sphere of what the *Qur'an* teaches, I'm blessed.

He talks animatedly about his three current challenges.

> I'm working on a web site course on the mystical dimension of Islamic tradition which deals with Islamic art and architecture as an expression of Islamic Spirituality. I'm also working on a project on Islamic law for Muslim physicians, which undertakes to investigate judicial rulings in the section of Islamic law that deals with issues of bioethics.

Another project is a comparative study of legal methodology in Islamic schools of legal thought. Sachedina is examining the work of Muslim jurists from five schools of Islamic law, four Sunni and one Shiite. Sachedina sits on more than a dozen advisory and editorial boards, including the *Encyclopedia of Ethics*, *Oxford Dictionary of Islam*, Center for Strategic and International Studies, *Journal of American Academy of Religion* and Tanenbaum Center for Interreligious Understanding.

Building Religious Inclusivity

March 2003

Religious inclusivity is not only a global ideal, but an important Canadian initiative. We live in perilous times where theories about a clash of civilizations abound. While the world has become a global village in terms of technology, travel and trade, the same strides are not seen in the world of faith.

It seems that the most troubled areas of the world are areas involved in religious conflict. Challenges faced by people of faith are enormous, but there is light at the end of the tunnel when we realize that "humanity is one community" (*Qur'an*), and many of our concerns are similar. As people of faith, we are all concerned about truth and justice, about poverty and violence and international human rights.

I believe the clash of civilizations can be averted if we can have communication between citizens of the earth. As theologian Hans Küng has said, "there can be no survival of democracy without a coalition of believers and non-believers in mutual respect."

How do we build mutual respect? In these challenging and too often troubled times, we need new perspectives and models so that we can find humane answers to the challenges of globalization, based on a deep respect for the diversity of cultures and religions in our world community. There is a desperate need for new and practical ways of reintroducing spirituality, ethics and faith into the international debate on globalization and the local consultation on inclusivity and social reform.

I believe that Canada is the model the world needs to emulate. I'm not alone in this thought. Karen Armstrong, prolific author and theologian, was invited to the launch of Women Engaging in Bridge Building on Parliament Hill, Ottawa, where she spoke about building bridges and religious inclusivity. Armstrong said that in her travels across the globe she has seen only one country where pluralism can work successfully. That country is Canada. I am energized to see *Time* magazine's recent cover story, entitled, A NATION AT PRAYER. I don't have to tell you which nation they are talking about but if you have any doubts, just look around you and tell me honestly, which other country in the world invites its multi-faith practitioners to a discussion about religious inclusivity in the heart of its political arena?

In this issue of *Time*, they write about a Vision TV/Time poll which finds that 84 percent of Canadians agree that all religions have elements of truth and three quarters believe that Canada's religious diversity is a source of strength for religious beliefs...that same diversity of religious experience in Canada may be increasing our tendency to explore faith. Furthermore, six out of 10 Canadians say they are interested in learning more about other religions and spiritual matters.

To illustrate this even better, I want share with you an email I received a few days ago. I don't know the writer but it warmed my heart, reinforcing my belief in the powers of religious diversity.

The gentleman writes:

Chapter 3: Truths of Islam

> Dear Ms. Raza:
> I received information that you are participating in a conference at the Episcopal Center in North Carolina at the end of January, 2004. My wife and I had the privilege of visiting Toronto recently and we met some really fine people there. I was really impressed by all the different racial and ethnic groups living in relative harmony, and at times felt like there was real brotherhood and sisterhood there. Yes, I thought Toronto was an exceptional place. Do you feel the same way about it? I am an American, born and raised in the Christian tradition, and a spiritual life is very important to me. I respect other religions as well. I am disturbed by the pointless hatred that is so prevalent in the world. As a person who wants to believe in the brotherhood of humanity despite all the evidence I see, if you think it would be worthwhile for me to attend, I will try to overcome some obstacles and come there to participate.

My answer to the writer and to you, my friends, is this:

Yes, you are right. While Toronto and Ontario are leaders in diversity, Canada overall is an exceptional multi-faith and multicultural mosaic. We have something quite unique in Canada and if we don't preserve, protect and promote it–we'll lose it. In the 14 years I've lived in Toronto, I've seen the growth of multi-faith groups and their freedom of religious expression. Canada has given protection to people of faith who were persecuted, sometimes in their country of birth. Here we live with freedom to practice our faith in any way we like. Differences in belief systems don't have to lead to confrontation.

In my tradition, we believe that unity of people doesn't necessarily mean their uniformity. So the unique concept of a garland of different flowers making a beautiful bouquet certainly personifies what Canada means to many of us.

Canada is being plugged as an international model of a pluralistic society. People will draw upon Canadian experience to help other societies engender pluralism in their institutions, laws and policies. Forming partnerships with Canada becomes valuable for institutions and individuals, who will serve as a strategic global source of values, knowledge, experience and practices of pluralism for diverse peoples from around the world. I have been invited to speak at three conferences in 2004, in the U.S., Dubai and Spain, to talk about what makes us tick. But we can't rest on our laurels. We still have a long way to go and need to practice what we preach.

> Nearly one quarter of Americans said they favoured making it illegal for Muslim groups to meet in the US for worship.

As the respected Dalai Lama said,

> It's not enough to belong to a religion. You also have to put it into practice. Religion is like a medicine. You have to ingest it to combat the illness.[28]

Speaking about illness, across the lakes and to the south of us, the waters are clearly murky. According

---

[28] Doogue, "Try Out Your Own Faith, Dalai Lama Tells Geneva Congregation."

to their own diversity survey, it was found that only 54 percent of the American public thinks all religions are equally true; 47 percent of respondents were of the view that the word "fanatical" applied to the religion of Islam. Nearly one quarter (23 percent) said they favored making it illegal for Muslim groups to meet in the U.S. for worship. While perceptions of Hindus and Buddhists were more favourable, one person in five still favored making it illegal for these groups to meet.

I can only say, Thank God for Canada, where pluralism is no longer a luxury, but has become a necessity of life. We have a choice. You may ask, what is religious inclusivity? As a Muslim, I could say that it means inclusion of my faith in the mainstream. The good news is that I do see inclusion of my faith. Imagine my surprise when after a decade of writing about Islam and Ramadhan, I walked past the Hudson's Bay Store on Toronto's Yonge Street and saw huge posters in the windows, saying Happy Ramadan. Similarly, IKEA has introduced décor for Muslim celebrations in their new brochure; the Ontario government gives Muslims vacation with pay for religious celebrations and schools reflect many of Islam's holy days.

This is a small start and I'm thrilled to see the transformation. Across the street from my home, a strip mall boasts of a halal meat shop alongside a lingerie store. This is the reality of pluralism in Canada. However, the religious inclusivity we are talking about here is not just acceptance of a few faiths; rather inclusion of all faith communities that make Canada their home because each faith brings valuable reflections and expands our understanding of the human community. If we want our faith to be reflected in the mainstream, then we must also lobby for other faiths.

I should add here that a significant imperative of religious inclusivity is to address our mutual concerns about social justice and social reform. Together, we can work towards our common goals of eliminating homelessness, child poverty, drugs, domestic violence and the pursuit of education reforms. These issues are important to all of us and transcend barriers of faith. United, we can have a strong voice and become a force for the government to contend with.

In our pursuit of justice, we must also recognize, accept and respect the majority tradition that this country was built upon. In our rush to build bridges, we must be cautious not to harm the foundation that's already in place. The Judeo-Christian values that Canada has upheld for decades are strong values and we can add to them–not eliminate them in order to promote our own agenda. Once we start the dialogue, we'll find we have more in common than differences.

Right now, we are heading into the Christmas and Hanukah season. These festivals must be acknowledged whether we religiously celebrate them or not. Let it be politically correct to say Merry Christmas, Happy Hanukah, Eid Mubarak or Happy Diwali, instead of lumping them all together under one generic greeting of Happy Holidays. We must make an effort to celebrate our differences because our long-term vision should not be one of just tolerating each other. Tolerance is not inclusive, it divides. What we want to achieve is acceptance, mutual harmony and working together towards the common good.

Critics would say this is impossible. I would offer that it's already happening on a small scale. Ten years ago, did you or I know what a multifaith or multicultural calendar was? No. But someone who cares about religious inclusivity has taken the time to reflect major faith celebrations in one joyful calendar.

In classrooms across Canada, various faiths are being recognized and celebrated. It would not be at all amiss, as far as I'm concerned, if in the public and private sector, in education and media, that a different faith is reflected, celebrated or acknowledged every day of the year. After all, students spend time and money to take a course in religions of the world. Here, all of us have the opportunity to learn about world religions without benefit of a university course.

Next, we come to the question of how religious inclusivity will take place. Can it be imposed by governments? I don't think so. Religious inclusivity only happens when faith communities and their leaders join hands with politicians to forge an understanding that through partnerships in a pluralistic society, we can encourage socially beneficial peace, nature-friendly behavior and affirming ecumenical decisions. To be sure, many people are already committing themselves to these goals, but a deeper change of consciousness is needed. Religious inclusivity has to be promoted from the pulpit. In places of worship, whether they are churches, temples, mosques or synagogues, the message should be one of pluralism and respect.

This will help us gain respect for each other and work on the basis of common visions, ideals, values, aims and criteria. This will also help us eliminate the seed of racism, which is ignorance. We have to understand that we have the power. We need the incentive to move beyond mere tolerance towards accepting all cultures and religions.

The Aga Khan, the spiritual leader of the Ismaili community, is in the process of building a centre for Pluralism in Canada. In his remarks about the importance of such an institution, he said,

> Fostering pluralism could be Canada's most powerful lever in enhancing its relations with all countries–in the Muslim world, in the larger developing world, and even in the West. Promoting pluralism provides an inclusive, sensitive approach to foreign relations. It means neither promulgating a single-faith/single-culture perspective, nor risking the perception that a single faith or society is being targeted for criticism. A focus on fostering pluralism would not only enhance relations between Canada and the Muslim world, it would also increase security and prosperity in Canada and around the world. Promoting pluralism could hold for Canada in the 21st century what peacekeeping held in the 20th century.

The World Parliament of Religions–Pathways to Peace

July 2004

There will be no peace among nations without peace among the religious.

Hans Küng

I had just finished performing my Friday prayers on the shores of the Mediterranean Sea. As I looked around me, I was filled with the wonder of being here, a long way from my native Pakistan and my adopted home, Canada.

I was in Barcelona to attend the Fourth Parliament of World Religions with two Canadian friends and partners in interfaith: Rev. Dr. Karen Hamilton, a practicing Christian, and Barbara Siddiqui, a practicing Muslim who was born in Ontario as a Christian.

It was an unusual situation in many ways. Two Caucasian women wearing shalwar qameez (Pakistani garb) were praying with me, along with a host of diverse Muslims in a VIP tent set up by the Sikh community of Birmingham, England. We were joined by local media keen to see how Muslims pray. (Thank God men and women prayed together that day!) The media were thoroughly confused when a turbaned Sikh and some non-Muslims came and joined the prayer.

This was interfaith at its best. The ad-hoc Imam said in his sermon, "Humanity is one community," and certainly at this point in time, anyone would agree.

The 2004 Parliament of World Religions was organized in partnership with the Universal Forum of Cultures–Barcelona 2004, which runs from May to September and in association with the UNESCO Centre of Catalonia. Eight thousand religious and spiritual practitioners from all over the world converged to greet and meet each other in peace. Four-hundred carefully selected seminars, workshops, performances and films were offered in the PWR program. They addressed three core themes: sustainable development, cultural diversity and conditions for peace through spiritual practice, religious identity and intra- and inter-religious dialogue. The Forum was supported by the presence of people like The Archbishop of Barcelona, Dr. Abdullah Omar Nasseef (President of the Muslim World Congress), Ela Gandhi (granddaughter of Mahatama Gandhi), Rabbi Henry J. Sobel (Chief Rabbi of Brazil) and many more. What was I doing there? I've been dabbling in interfaith dialogue since I moved to Canada in 1989, but September 11 threw me into the heart of interfaith dialogue. In 2003, I saw a call for papers for PWR. I immediately contacted my partners in interfaith dialogue, Karen and Barbara, and said, "I'm going. Are you coming with me?" They were thrilled at the opportunity.

Of course, the fact that the venue was Barcelona only added to our desire to be there. We worked together on a proposal titled *Keeping the Path Clear–Women Engaging in Inter-faith, Inter-action and Inter-*

relationships. By June, 2004, we hadn't heard back from PWR but we decided to go anyway. At the end of June, I was looking through the online program and I found our names. Our proposal had been accepted!

For me, this was a journey from the heart. Whenever I read or talked about Muslim history, I used to imagine the rich Muslim, Jewish and Christian heritage of Spain, when the three faiths lived in harmony and reached out to each other spiritually and intellectually. Here was a chance to promote that same essence of pluralism and I felt especially blessed to be chosen for this opportunity. It was only later I discovered how fortunate we were to be selected from among the thousands of proposals that were submitted.

On our first day in Barcelona, Barb, Karen and I took the metro to the Forum site. On the metro we met a South Asian couple wearing PWR badges and we chatted. As we exchanged names, the lady said, "So you are Raheel Raza?" I was a bit shocked. She was the vice president of PWR and she knew me through our proposal, which she said she personally approved because there weren't too many Muslim women presenters from North America. We were thrilled and humbled at the same time, to be invited to present along with theologians like Hans Küng and Tariq Ramadan, Nobel Peace Prize laureate Adolfor Perez Esquivel (the Portuguese writer), activists like Susan George and authors like Deepak Chopra. This was a gift.

The Forum site was a 30-hectare space next to the Mediterranean Sea and an extension of the waterfront that began with the 1992 Olympic Games.

It was a sight for sore eyes and hearts. There was a sea of people in the colors of the world; dresses, voices, faces of diversity. The orange robes of Buddhist monks mingled with the white dresses of the Sufis. Everyone stopped and wished each other in peace, smiled and sometimes spontaneously hugged each other. This was beyond tolerance; it was embracing each other.

Throughout the Forum site there were four major exhibitions, 22 smaller shows, 400 concerts, 170 music groups, 60 street performances and four circuses. Everywhere were interactive installations, markets, games and fun. High-tech, well organized events manned by hundreds of youth volunteers from all over the world were exceptional. Our trio caused some surprise. A yogi nun from America told me she had never met such strong Muslim women before and she hoped we would change the world!

Shirin Ebadi, 2003 Nobel Peace Prize laureate, stated in the opening of the Parliament of the World's Religions, "Human rights cannot be protected with bombs" and denounced the despotic behavior of those "who ignore human rights and democracy with the argument of belonging to a different culture and shadow dictatorial regimes with religious and nationalistic arguments."

In her address speech, Ebadi defended Islam, declaring it is compatible with respect for human rights and democracy by showing the Islamic Declaration of Human Rights. In her opinion, "if each of the 5,000 religions of the world made their own declaration, this would be the end of the Universal Declaration of Human Rights."

She went on to say, "God has made human beings different but the ultimate goal of all religions is the pursuit of happiness and thus all religions can share the things they have in common."

We attended as many dialogue sessions as we could, sometimes together and other times separately. But we always met for lunch at the same place, The Parliament by the Sea. This was a tent city set up on the seashore of the sea by the Sikh community of Birmingham, U.K. Here, volunteers from the Sikh community, ages 16 to 60, first welcomed people, then poured water on their hands, gave people headscarves and served lunch, drinks and water. They catered to nearly 6,000 people each day. They also invited participants to pray in their scared spaces tent. My longing for *desi* food was quenched with *pooris* (fried bread), *daal* (lentils), *chawal* (rice) and *achaar* (pickle).

Our presentation was slotted for Saturday, July 10 at 11:30 a.m. We arrived there early, nervous because we had no way of knowing how many people would attend. To our delight, a trustee from PWR came to introduce our session and told us how important it was to acknowledge the work we are doing. We felt honored. Our room soon filled with diverse people, including some Barcelona Muslims. Karen, Barb and I spoke about the interfaith work we do and why we do it. At the end of our session, we distributed little boxes containing a Canadian maple syrup candy, a Canada pin and a message saying "Pray for Peace–Act for Peace", while we played Dawud Wharnsaby's song called People of the Boxes from the CD, The Prophet's Hands.

Later, people came up to ask us questions. A man wearing an Arab dress and a kufi, came to me, blessed me for the work we do and to my surprise, had tears running down his face as he said, "You make me proud to be Muslim." It wasn't the only time in Barcelona that I felt touched to tears.

The same evening, the City of Barcelona had arranged for "A Communities Night", so that people of faith could meet their own communities in different parts of the city. Barbara and I went to Ramlas Raval and met the Barcelona Muslim community. There is a large Arab and Pakistani community active in Barcelona and the Imams of two mosques gave talks condemning violence and terrorism, which was heartening to hear. We learned that after the Madrid train bombing, people of all faiths had joined together in Barcelona, engaging in candlelight vigils for peace.

> In this awe-inspiring structure, ten religious traditions presented music, movement, meditation and chants.

On the following night, there was a Sacred Music concert at the Sagrada Familia (The Sacred Family) Cathedral, which is one of the most outstanding landmarks of Barcelona. It was built by renowned architect Antoni Gaudi and is still unfinished. In this awe-inspiring structure, 10 religious traditions presented music, movement, meditation and chants. It was an unforgettable experience, sitting under the clear skies while the cathedral resonated with the sounds of the Cor Gospel of Barcelona; Ang singing from India; Sheva, a Jewish-Muslim band with roots in Hebrew, Arabic and Tribal cultures and Ushaq, the rich musical legacy of the Sufi Mevlevi order. As the Sufis started chanting Allah Hu, there was a hush, and then a few people joined in and I trembled as I heard more than half the audience chanting with the Sufis. The concert ended with 10 children of 10 traditions holding up peace lights.

After a week of debates centered on commitments on the issues of religious violence, access to safe water, the fate of refugees worldwide and the elimination of developing countries' debts, the PWR came to a close. Religious leaders who convened the gathering deemed the event a success. Dirk Ficca, executive director of the Council for PWR, said that one fundamental difference between this gathering and others discussing the same subjects was this:

> When people of faith commit to address religious violence and other pressing issues facing the global community, they follow through. We make a commitment not only to the world, but out of a deeply rooted religious or spiritual conviction. That is what makes the Barcelona Parliament commitments so special, and why this year's Parliament in Barcelona is going to make an impact.

Beyond the Fluff Stuff

September 2004

We live in times that boggle our minds and try our souls. Times when a culture of hatred has taken precedence over our traditions of peace, love and tolerance. Usually, a sentence that begins with the words "an Imam, a Rabbi and a Priest..." is the opening line of a joke. These days, the grouping of religions is a serious matter.

It is empowering to see that institutions like churches and mosques are taking the initiative to know each other. We need more open doors. Interfaith needs to be done at an individual level, in every aspect of our lives. Faith leaders should lead the way and talk more about the interfaith objective at every opportunity. For Muslims, knowing their spiritual neighbors is an inherent part of the faith.

A specific process needs to be put into place through workshops or seminars, where Muslims can be given guidelines on how to participate in interfaith.

Why is guidance necessary when interfaith relations are built into the Muslim faith? Through my own experience, I've learned this: Interfaith is not everyone's cup of tea.

There is an old Arabic proverb: words from lips reach the ears, but words from the heart reach the heart. Interfaith has to come from the heart.

Some people think that interfaith is a competition and take an aggressive stance: My god is better than your god. They believe interfaith is not for them.

As Karen Armstrong, who calls herself a freelance monotheist, says so beautifully, "We need humility before knowledge–we have to kill our ego and only then can sincere and true interfaith take place."

Knowledge, also known as a weapon of mass instruction, is essential to interfaith dialogue. This knowledge is not only of those we think of as "the other" but also of ourselves. Intra-faith dialogue needs to happen alongside inter-faith dialogue. If we don't know ourselves, how can we extend ourselves to others outside our tradition?

In guiding our community towards interfaith, the first step is to create trust. Trust comes when we look for commonalities and similarities. I have met people who think interfaith means highlighting the differences in faith traditions. While there is no compromising of principles, I believe that all faith traditions have a lot more in common than they have differences. It's just easier to point out the differences. But when we take the time and effort to talk about similarities, it builds trust, educates and informs.

Once we establish trust, we need to move to a higher level of dialogue which I call Beyond the Fluff Stuff. It is not just discussion about religious holidays, but ongoing dialogue about some of the more difficult issues which we don't wish to sweep under the table but need to debate in a civilized manner in an atmosphere of respect and trust.

For example, my group of interfaith women did a panel of the parts of our scriptures that we have difficulty in interpreting. We discovered that in the three monotheistic traditions, our concerns were similar, so we began to relate at a different level of understanding.

I have a bumper sticker on my car that says "Those who pray together stay together." This is an important discovery on the journey to interfaith. How often do we pray together?

In Barcelona, Spain, at the Parliament of World Religions in 2004, we did pray together. Praying together removes insecurity and fear and helps people understand that interfaith does not mean conversion.

> Praying together removes insecurity and fear and helps people understand that interfaith does not mean conversion.

Further to knowledge, I have a recommendation for Canada's educational system. I believe some study of religion needs to be made part of the curriculum in junior schools. I know there are a few groups working towards this and I support their initiative because even in secular terms, this is about the history of the world. I know comparative religion is taught in high school but I think that is rather late. In the Canadian mosaic, children are exposed to diverse faiths every day of their lives (except those in very isolated and elite private educational systems), so an understanding of other faiths can only create tolerance and respect.

Faith is a four letter word in the media, so interfaith doesn't make good news because it is warm and fuzzy and brings people together, which doesn't sell newspapers. Note how much coverage a racial or religiously motivated crime will get as compared to an event such as the Parliament of World Religions in Barcelona. It was the largest interfaith gathering in the world and barely made international news. We have to empower media to support the interfaith work happening at many levels and write to our local media about such events.

We must also understand that interfaith is not a one-time solution. Neither is it a band-aid solution. It needs to be worked at consistently, persistently and continuously to make a difference in a world that has been torn by religious strife.

Three Weddings and a Funeral
MAY 2004

At a Muslim wedding in Markham recently, about 350 guests faced an embarrassing situation. The self-proclaimed Imam (spiritual leader) who was invited by the hosts to say a few words got totally carried away and gave a long, offensive monologue. First, he publicly denounced non- Muslims for lacking family values; he asked the groom thrice if he wanted to escape from the wedding; furthermore he informed the bride that she does not have the right to step outside the house or give anything to her family without her husband's permission. He reinforced these "rules" by mentioning hellfire and brimstone. There was no talk of love, respect and consideration between the couple. The guests were stunned, the couple looked shocked and a few people stood up in protest but no one contradicted the speaker. Obviously, they had no idea what to do.

Upon inquiring how a balanced, educated family could allow someone to spew such vitriol, the hosts explained their agreement with the speaker had been for him to repeat the marriage sermon of Prophet Mohammad as done traditionally at Muslim weddings (which is short and simple, highlighting the sanctity and beauty of marriage). They had no clue that he would indulge in histrionics.

Muslim marriages do not necessitate a sermon to be recited as part of the religious ceremony. The requirement is for *aqd*, which is solemnization of the contract through offering and acceptance with full and free consent of the parties concerned, two witnesses and a gift from the groom to the bride. A respected community member may be invited to say a few words, which could range from relevant verses of the *Qur'an* to Sufi poetry by Rumi. A public celebration to bless the union is considered to be Sunnah (practice of the Prophet) and this celebration can be as festive as the family wishes it to be. Weddings are not meant to be dark and dreary as some dysfunctional Mullahs indicate, when they pose themselves as reformers, exhorting misogynist theories supported by useless traditions and ranting about "Western corruption", which is absolutely contrary to the faith.

It seems these people have taken it upon themselves to use occasions like weddings and funerals to endorse their personal views. Recently, at a funeral in Toronto, the Imam who was asked to pray for the soul of the departed blasted the Supreme Court of Canada for 30 minutes on the issue of same sex marriages! Wrong time, wrong place.

However, misuse of power by religious leaders is not unique to the Muslim community. In Santa Fe, New Mexico, a family has filed a lawsuit against their local Catholic church over a funeral mass in which the priest allegedly said their relative was a "lukewarm" Catholic and was going to hell. (*The Toronto Star*, July 18, 2003). Religious exploitation seems to have taken the world by storm.

At a second wedding in Toronto, the Imam lectured women about their marital duties, interpreted in the most conservative framework, with no mention that Prophet Mohammad's wife, Khadija, a suc-

Chapter 3: Truths of Islam

cessful businesswoman, had sent a proposal of marriage to him. He then informed the guests that they shouldn't befriend Jews and Christians and proceeded to point out the faults of the "infidels" until the young bride burst into tears and told him that most of her friends present at the event were Jews and Christians! So much for joy!

Our only hope as a thriving and contributing Canadian Muslim community lies in removing the power of those who distort the faith. Some young Muslims took the initiative of doing just that at a recent wedding. The bride and her brother organized the reception, informing the parents that their only contribution would be their credit card! There was no sermon. The occasion reflected the best of both Muslim and Western worlds. Point

> Family and friends were invited to a mixed reception where hijab and henna mingled with halter dresses and high heels to the strains of traditional music.

of note is the families of the bride and groom are quite traditional, so a simple religious ceremony had been performed earlier at a mosque with immediate family in attendance. Later, family and friends were invited to a mixed reception where hijab and henna mingled with halter dresses and high heels to the strains of traditional music. Friends and families blessed the couple in an atmosphere filled with joy– finally, a Muslim-Canadian wedding with some feeling.

What Led to the London Bombings?

July 2005

The heart-rending loss of humanity in the wake of the London, England bombings is a tragedy that affects all of us, Muslim and non-Muslim alike.

The blasts didn't come as a total surprise because the writing was on the wall. Despite the cause and effect theory, which has been propounded extensively by commentators, this is a home-grown problem and it can only be solved within the community that allowed it to grow. That community is not necessarily a religious community, but a multicultural community like ours here in Canada.

I say this with feeling because I am a Pakistani Muslim woman with two sons, the same age as the suicide bombers in London. The difference is that my sons are secular in their public life and soundly knowledgeable and religious in their private life. They have grown up in an environment of respect for interfaith and life. More importantly, they know how to balance both.

Early this year, my 20-year-old son, Saif, went to Birmingham, England to visit a friend he hadn't seen in a long time. When he returned he was quite perturbed. Upon probing, he confessed that he found his counterparts in England very disturbing in their religious ideology. Attending Friday prayer in a mosque, Saif was shocked by the fire and brimstone being spouted from the pulpit.

Later, he took a drive with his Muslim friend. They had a flat tire. My son noted they had just passed a gas station and suggested they take the car there to be fixed. To his surprise and dismay, the three British-Muslim boys with him said they would rather walk than take their business to a non-Muslim. They proceeded to try and indoctrinate my son about the ills of the West and how important it was not to integrate with locals. Saif was alarmed by the attitude of these young Muslims and found they were totally dishonest and disconnected with the reality of living in the West and with any values of assimilation.

I've seen this trend on my visits to Britain. There is a growing sense of frustration in the youth and it's dangerous. The London bombings are symbolic of this malaise.

Granted, there are many political, economic and social factors that come into play when we talk about terrorism today. These are not part of a hidden agenda any more. Anyone with half a brain is aware that the war in Iraq and the American foreign policy play strong roles in any reaction to the West. But it does not, and will never, justify death of innocents. Can this happen in Canada? Maybe. Unless we wake up and smell the coffee. By "we", I don't mean only Muslims, although public opinion would like to make this exclusively an Islamic problem. When the bubble of complacency bursts, it affects all of us. Before we are left blaming each other, let's try and look at solutions.

CHAPTER 3: TRUTHS OF ISLAM 167

I don't believe technical surveillance, airport checks, limiting immigration and picking up bearded Muslim men at random is the solution. Obviously, targeting one community is not the answer, either. The solution lies with parents and guardians, peers and advisors, teachers and religious institutions. All of us need to be more vigilant about the kind of rhetoric being spouted, about the ideology of hate being exported into Canada, about Muslim youth becoming targets for al-Qaeda recruiters in places of education and worship. Most important perhaps, is teaching our youth to raise their voices in condemning all acts of violence and being aware about what is going on around them.

> All of us need to be more vigilant about the kind of rhetoric being spouted, about the ideology of hate... about Muslim youth becoming targets for al-Qaeda recruiters... Most important perhaps, is teaching our youth to raise their voices in condemning all acts of violence.

Last month, two of the largest centres of Islamic learning, Al Azhar in Egypt and Qum in Iran, issued a joint fatwa, stating that suicide bombing is a sin–an unacceptable act under any circumstance. In Amman, Jordan, more than 170 Muslim scholars, thinkers and historians who gathered for an international Islamic conference agreed to forbid labeling anyone with apostasy, condemning extremists who use hate ideology to fire up sentiments against others.

In response to those who want to know where moderate Muslims are hiding, let me inform them we are alive and well and working around the clock to undo the damage done by 30 years of indoctrination of an ideology of hate. Where and how this ideology was invited into the West is a whole other story, but let it suffice to say that we work hard to get our voices heard. But like every other extremist movement, the loudest voices are those of the damned.

The bombing in London was close to home. My brother-in-law was on the train just before the one that was bombed. We were terrified till we knew he was safe. Similarly, hundreds of other relatives, friends and loved ones must also have worried themselves sick. In the wake of the attack, many families mourn their dead and so do we.

Our loss increases as we mourn not only the dead and wounded, we also mourn the living who have lost their souls. Before the soul of our faith, our youth, our loved ones, is sucked away by the devil in disguise, let us join hands for the greatest of all jihads–the struggle to respect the dignity of human life.

Eid and Awe in New York

March 2005

Eid. A word that means joy. It's the feast after the fast, a major celebration for Muslims after fasting in the month of Ramadan. Deciding to spend Eid in New York this past weekend turned out to be a joyous decision on my part, and while tradition has it that Eid lasts for three days, I celebrated in a variety of ways for the whole week.

But I'm getting ahead of myself.

I went to NYC ostensibly to attend the launch of the Progressive Muslims Union of North America. I arrived two days early. My hosts in Manhattan are part of a group that had decided that through science and technology, Ramadan and Eid can be predicted in advance of physical moon sighting, so that Muslims can begin and end together. The decision was for a Sunday Eid and they invited me to join them at the Eid prayer and celebration.

We drove to the Dorral Arrowood Convention Center in Rye Brook, New York, where the auspicious event was arranged by the American Sufi Muslim Association (ASMA). Three-hundred men, women and children prayed together in the great ballroom, side by side, with no partition. These people have broken away from the traditional mosque culture (where usually women are relegated to another area) because they want to offer prayers with their families, friends and loved ones. They took another bold step by inviting an Imam of their choice. And what a brilliant choice!

Imam Feisal Abdul Rauf is a dynamic man with a vision as large as his heart.[29] Author of a new book titled, *What's Right with Islam: A New Vision for Muslims in the West,* he was educated in England and Malaysia and has a degree in physics from Columbia University. Founder and CEO of ASMA and Imam of Masjid Al-Farah, a mosque in New York City, twelve blocks from Ground Zero, Imam Feisal has dedicated his life to building bridges between Muslims and the West. He is a leader in the effort to build religious pluralism and integrate Islam into modern American society.

Regarded as one of the world's most eloquent and erudite Muslim leaders, Imam Feisal is a charismatic public speaker and has appeared in national and international media, including CNN, CBS, NBC, ABC, PBS and BBC. He has been quoted in The New York Times, New York Daily News, Jerusalem Post and Associated Press.

The Imam's sermon could have been easily accepted in a church, synagogue or temple as he spoke about two kinds of religion–good and bad. He talked about Islam with a small "i" and said it means submission to God by anyone: Muslim, Christian, Jew, Buddhist. This must have sat well with John Bennet, a lone Buddhist in the congrega-

---

[29] As mentioned in the *Introduction*, Imam Rauf is heading the construction of the controversial Ground Zero mosque, which Raheel so very much opposes. Her opinion of him has fallen far from where it was when she wrote this article. At the very least, this disagreement illustrates that Islam is neither static nor monolithic.

tion who heads the Cordoba Initiative. Imam Feisal is the architect of the Cordoba Initiative, an inter-religious blueprint for improving relations between America and the Muslim world and pursuing Middle East peace. As a tireless advocate for an ecumenical solution to the Israeli-Palestinian conflict, he has impressed his vision on U.S. lawmakers and administration officials, most recently as member of the National Inter-religious Initiative for Peace in Washington, D.C.

Young people surrounded the Imam after the sermon, which was unusual in itself, but the surprise did not end there for me. Following the prayer, there was brunch and live music. Some enthusiastic families also indulged in a bit of bhangra (Punjabi disco). I was also astounded to see that the Imam's wife, Daisy Khan, does not cover her head. She leads women in prayer at their mosque and is involved in interfaith dialogue at an international level. Upon my questioning, she said, "I've done my own *ijtihad* (research and reasoning) and found that modest dress is what is required so I believe this is fine for me."

> The Imam's wife, Daisy Khan, does not cover her head. She leads women in prayer at their mosque and is involved in interfaith dialogue...

I had definitely encountered progressive Muslims.

The next morning, Monday, November 15, was the official launch of *The Progressive Muslims Union of North America*. The Union Theological Seminary of Columbia University hosted this event in the Bonheoffer Room (at one time called The Prophet's Chamber).

PMU is the result of months of work and planning by a diverse group of American Muslims, including renowned academics such as Omid Safi, professor of Islamic Studies at Colgate University. Professionals like Hussein Ibish, communications director of the American-Arab Anti-Discrimination Committee and Sarah Eltantawi, a consultant to American organizations and communication director for PMU. There were also community activists like Ahmed Nassef, editor-in-chief of Muslim Wakeup, the world's most popular Muslim online magazine.

Sarah Eltantawi opened the media event by saying, "PMU seeks to expand the range of spiritual, social, intellectual and political choices for North American Muslims, and to challenge the narrow set of "normative" Muslim ideas and behavior expected of all of us both within and beyond the North American Muslim community." When asked if they are a breakaway group, she responded that the aim is not to create some sort of "new Islam" or "American Islam".

> Rather, we seek to join the work already underway by so many others to bolster the sense of pluralism, commitment to justice, and diversity within Islamic discourses which has been undermined by the spread of literalist and dogmatic interpretations of the faith in recent decades.

Ahmed Nassef spoke about the four different areas that PMU will work in: arts, reform and education; spiritual awareness; and politics. He said that PMU is like a "big tent" under which they hope other ex-

Chapter 3: Truths of Islam

isting organizations will gather to defend civil rights at home, human rights abroad and celebrate an enlightened vision of Islam.

Joining the PMU board is Torontonian Tarek Fatah, founder of the Muslim Canadian Congress, who pointed out that Canada has made great contributions to the progressive religions agenda. He started off by stating, "Canada has more to offer the U.S. than just cheap drugs for seniors. Canadians don't just pay lip service but actually practice a separation of religion and state". MCC will pursue the Canadian component of the progressive Muslim agenda here at home, not without controversy. Tarek had hardly arrived home when he was slapped with the label of being a "progressive extremist" (whatever that means).

During my interaction with other American Muslims over Eid celebrations, I heard some criticism of PMU. One was that they might compromise basic Islamic principles and "pander to western popular ideology". Others referred to this group as "being too liberal" because they feel the PMU mandate is too wide. The PMU board seemed well aware of the challenges ahead of them and said they expect the community will go through denial, anger and then hopefully acceptance when they see there is a need for reform from within.

A New York Times columnist who had come to cover the event commented that the kind of message being given by PMU through their mission statement is a discourse that is not heard in the mainstream and felt it is important to get the message out.

I found the PMU board very sincere in their efforts to try and find a balance. I fully support their mandate for exorcizing the excesses of many within the community who veer towards polemics and hate propaganda, which has no place in our faith. I applaud their decision to avoid extremism of every kind and to be inclusive, respecting the diversity of our faith, culture and traditions. My only concern is that in labeling themselves "progressive" or "moderate", is the message being given to the outside world that those who aren't part of any such organization are not progressive or moderate?

> The columnist made note that none of the women who attended the PMU launch were wearing hijab. This bothers me because the message seems to connect head covering with being regressive and that is certainly not the case.

The New York Times columnist made note that none of the women who attended the PMU launch were wearing hijab. This bothers me because the message seems to connect head covering with being regressive and that is certainly not the case.

Another news item in mainstream media talked about young Muslims becoming extremist by "going regularly to the mosque, growing a beard and wearing Islamic attire." By this standard, the majority of Muslims, including my own two sons, could easily be labeled extremist. I feel some caution is needed to ensure the medium does not mangle the message!

Upon returning to Toronto, I encountered my own pluralistic experience. I am teaching an eight-part series on "Understanding Islam" to a group called Learning Unlimited, which is comprised of 200 educated Canadians, mostly Christian and some secular. This week, the presentation was on spirituality in Islam and sharing the stage with me was a Sufi who is a holocaust survivor from Hungary. This man of Jewish heritage led the entire audience in zikr of Allah and His Prophet, explained the concept of Sufism better than I could ever have done, read poetry by Rumi and Rabia al Basri, and submitted to questions till he was exhausted. It was incredible to see this crowd, some who had never said the word Allah in their lives, chanting the kalima, not once but repeatedly. Later, some people came to me and said this was the first time they were spiritually touched and requested the words to be written down for them.

So, my faith reinforced, my energies recharged and my spirit rejuvenated over Ramadan and Eid, I wish to share my enlightenment with you:

If it's not moderate, progressive, enlightening, delightful or tolerant, then it's not Islam.

A FREE GIFT
from Raheel*

Whereas, Westerners, in centuries past, have willfully engaged in many wars against people of the Islamic faith,

Whereas, Westerners do currently engage in open war against countries which are predominantly Muslim,

Whereas, the leaders of Western governments have acted in a clumsy and ignorant fashion (whether attempting diplomacy or war) toward governments of predominantly Muslim lands,

Therefore, Westerners and their ancestors have been guilty of predjudice and gross ignorance regarding the life and teachings of Mohammed and of Muslims themselves.

But, in recognition that Westerners have been victims of predjudice, mass murder and clumsy diplomacy at the hands of Muslims,

I, Raheel Raza, do grant permission, to all who are curious about Islam, that you may satisfy your curiosity by actually seeking answers.

Therefore, on behalf of Muslims far and wide, when you find yourself among us, near us or otherwise dealing with us and you are uncertain about how to act, what to say or what to think, you have my everlasting "thumbs up", to come right out... and ASK.

Raheel Raza
Gracious and Generous Grantor

---

* This was quite directly inspired by economist and syndicated columnist Walter E. Williams, whose own gift is located at
http://econfaculty.gmu.edu/wew/gift.html

Brief Islamic Glossary

Adl	Justice
Allah	God
Ayat	Parables
Bhangra	Punjabi disco
Eid	The feast after the fast
Fatwa	Non-binding religious decree
Gurdwara	Place of worship for Sikhs
Hijab	Female Head covering
Kalima	Testimony of faith: "There is no God but God and Mohammad is His Messenger"
Kufi	Male head covering
Imam	Leader
Khutbah	Sermon
Ijtehad	Independent, individual thought
Ijma	Community consensus
Munafiq	Hypocrite
Qur'an	The Muslim Holy Book
Ramadhan	Month of fasting
Shahadah	Testimony of Faith
Shaitan	Devil
Sunnah	Practice of the Prophet
Surah	Verse
Ulema	Religious scholars
Zikr	Remembrance

Bibliography

A Filmmaking Odyssey: The Making of Journey of Faith. DVD. Timpanogos Entertainment, 2006.

Armstrong, Karen. *A History of God: The 4,000-Year Quest of Judaism, Christianity and Islam*. Softcover Ed. Ballantine Books, 1994.

— — —. "Fundamentalism and the Secular Society." *International Journal* 59, no. 4 (October 1, 2004): 875–877. www.jstor.org/stable/40203988.

Bakhtiar, Laleh. *Shariati on Shariati and the Muslim Woman*. Kazi Publications, 1996.

Brown, S. Kent, and Peter Johnson, eds. *Journey of Faith: From Jerusalem to the Promised Land*. Hardcover. BYU: Neal A. Maxwell Institute for Religious School, 2006.

Chittick, William C. *The Sufi Path of Love: The Spiritual Teachings of Rumi*. State University of New York Press, 1983.

Diamond, Jared M. *Collapse: How Societies Choose to Fail or Succeed*. 1st Paperback. Penguin (Non-Classics), 2005.

Doogue, Edmund. "Try Out Your Own Faith, Dalai Lama Tells Geneva Congregation." *Ecumenical News International Feature*, August 10, 1999. http://gbgm-umc.org/europe/switzerland/eni081099edmw.html.

Emel Magazine. "When Muslims Saved Jews." *Emel - The Muslim Lifestyle Magazine*, January 2010. www.emel.com/article?id=67&a_id=1788.

Evans, Derek. *Before the War: Reflections in a New Millennium*. Wood Lake Publishing Inc., 2004.

Fadl, Khaled Abou El. *Speaking in God's Name: Islamic Law, Authority and Women*. First ed. Oneworld Publications, 2001.

Feiler, Bruce. *Abraham: A Journey to the Heart of Three Faiths*. Harper Perennial, 2005.

Gershman, Norman. *Besa: Muslims Who Saved Jews in World War II*. 1st ed. Syracuse N.Y.: Syracuse University Press, 2008.

Hassan, Riffat. *Women's Rights and Islam: From the I. C. P. D. to Beijing*. Privately Printed C. 1995, 1111.

Hussain, Dr. Amir. *Security and Preparedness*. Chautauqua, 2007. http://fora.tv/2007/08/10/Security_and_Preparedness_Dr__Amir_Hussain.

Lacey, Marc. "Rwandan Priest Sentenced to 15 Years for Allowing Deaths of Tutsi in Church." *The New York Times*, December 14, 2006, sec. International / Africa. www.nytimes.com/2006/12/14/world/africa/14rwanda.html.

Lang, Jeffrey. *Losing My Religion: A Call For Help*. amana, 2004.

Mernissi, Fatima. *Beyond the Veil, Revised Edition: Male-Female Dynamics in Modern Muslim Society*. Revised ed. Indiana University Press, 1987.

Mir-Hosseini, Ziba. *Islam and Gender*. Princeton University Press, 1999.

Ngowi, Rodrique. "Rwanda Turns To Islam After Genocide." *The Herald Tribune*, November 10, 2002. http://muslimvillage.com/story.php?id=705.

Nieuwoudt, Stephanie. "Rwanda: Church Role in Genocide Under Scrutiny." *Institute for War & Peace Reporting*, no. ACR Issue 85 (December 1, 2006). www.iwpr.net/report-news/rwanda-church-role-genocide-under-scrutiny.

"Nun Convicted for Rwandan Genocide." *The Associated Press*, November 10, 2006. www.msnbc.msn.com/id/15653352/.

"Raheel Raza Interviewed on The O'Reilly Factor About Her Opposition to the Ground Zero Mosque." *The O'Reilly Factor*. Fox News, August 9, 2010. http://youtu.be/KHg9gzo9o-U.

Ruelle, Karen Gray, and Deborah Durland Desaix. *The Grand Mosque of Paris: A Story of How Muslims Rescued Jews During the Holocaust*. Reprint. Holiday House, 2010.

Sachedina, Abdulaziz. *The Islamic Roots of Democratic Pluralism*. Oxford University Press, USA, 2007.

Safi, Omid. *Progressive Muslims: On Justice, Gender, and Pluralism*. Oneworld Publications, 2003.

Schwartz, Stephen. "Terrorism Has a Name - Wahhabism." News. *Free Republic*, October 5, 2001. www.freerepublic.com/focus/f-news/540730/posts.

— — —. *The Two Faces of Islam: Saudi Fundamentalism and Its Role in Terrorism*. First. Anchor, 2003.

Soroush, Abdolkarim. *Reason, Freedom, and Democracy in Islam: Essential Writings of Abdolkarim Soroush*. Oxford University Press, USA, 2002.

Steyn, Mark. *America Alone: The End of the World as We Know It*. Hardcover. Regnery Publishing, Inc., 2006.

Tantawi, Muhammad Sayyid. "View from the Occident." *Agence France Presse*, November 14, 2001. http://occident.blogspot.com/2009/07/islam-muslims-question-of-violence.html.

Tucker, Judith E. *In the House of the Law: Gender and Islamic Law in Ottoman Syria and Palestine*. 1st ed. University of California Press, 2000.

Wadud, Amina. *Qur'an and Woman: Rereading the Sacred Text from a Woman's Perspective*. Oxford University Press, USA, 1999.

About the Author

Raheel Raza is a public speaker, Consultant for Interfaith and Intercultural diversity, documentary filmmaker, freelance journalist and founder of Sacred Arts ad Music Alliance.

Raza bridges the gap between East and West, promoting cultural and religious diversity. She has appeared in print, on television and radio to discuss diversity, harmony and interfaith. In a presentation to Members of Parliament and international diplomats at the House of Commons, Raza received a standing ovation for her speech called "Celebrating our Differences".

An outspoken advocate for gender equality and an activist for women's rights internationally, she has appeared many times in print, radio and television media to reveal and debate Canadian issues related to media, diversity, gender and immigrants. Raza has received many awards for her work to build bridges of understanding. She is a recipient of the City of Toronto's Constance Hamilton Award and is the first South Asian woman to narrate a CBC documentary on "Passionate Eye". A fervent advocate for human rights, Raza is the first Muslim woman in Canada to lead mixed gender prayers.

(continued on next page)

Growing up in a culture where women were supposed to "be seen and not heard", Raza turned to writing at a young age and is a freelance journalist. Traveling extensively throughout the world, Raza brings a fresh global perspective to her mandate "there is unity in diversity". Raza has spoken at places of worship, the private sector, the Justice Department, School Boards and government institutions. She has also been invited to speak at Universities in USA and Canada, including Harvard and Columbia.

www.ingramcontent.com/pod-product-compliance
Lightning Source LLC
LaVergne TN
LVHW051519070426
835507LV00023B/3187